IS THE BIBLE THE INERRANT WORD OF GOD?

R. A. TORREY

IS THE BIBLE THE INERRANT WORD OF GOD

AND

WAS THE BODY OF JESUS RAISED FROM THE DEAD

BY

R. A. TORREY

DEAN, BIBLE INSTITUTE, LOS ANGELES

*Author of "The Importance and Value of Proper Bible Study,"
"The Real Christ," "What the Bible Teaches,"
"How to Work for Christ," etc.*

PUBLISHERS
Eugene, Oregon

Wipf and Stock Publishers
199 W 8th Ave, Suite 3
Eugene, OR 97401

Is the Bible the Inerrant Word of God
and Was the Body of Jesus Raised from the Dead
By Torrey, R.A.
ISBN: 1-59244-812-7
Publication date 8/26/2004
Previously published by George Doran, 1922

INTRODUCTION

Three great questions are agitating the church today, and seem likely to divide it. The three great questions are: First, Is the Bible the Inerrant Word of God? Second, Was the body of Jesus that was nailed to the Cross and really died, raised from the dead? Third, was Jesus born of a Virgin? The first two of these questions are the more fundamental, but the third is of great importance. Of course, if it can be shown that the Bible is the Inerrant Word of God, the question of the Virgin Birth of our Lord is also settled. In this book we have taken up the first and second questions. The reader will have to judge for himself whether we have answered the questions satisfactorily or not.

There is in the church today a wide-spread opinion that the Bible is not the Word of God, but simply *"contains the Word of God,"* and that it is very far from inerrant. This opinion is held not only by some prominent ministers in the various evangelical churches but by a considerable number of professors in theological seminaries in the Evangelical denominations where men are being trained for the ministry at home and for foreign missionary work abroad; and it is the opinion of many competent judges that our whole evangelistic work at home and our missionary work abroad is seriously threatened by the growth of this opinion.

INTRODUCTION

Within the past few years there has been, one almost might say, a "broad-casting" among Evangelical ministers of a view of the Resurrection of Jesus Christ which is entirely different from that given in the Bible. Those who hold this view say that they believe in the Resurrection of Jesus Christ; but, if pressed, they frankly confess that by the Resurrection of Jesus Christ they do not mean the resurrection of His body, but a spiritual resurrection, a resurrection of His spirit. This view is also taught not merely in the theological seminaries of some of the so-called "Liberal" denominations, but in the theological seminaries of denominations that have always been held to be Evangelical. The writer was surprised to discover last summer how this opinion had grown among missionaries in China. There is certainly great need that this question also be faced and dealt with thoroughly. This we have endeavored to do in this book. If something is not done of a definite, decided and effective character to stem the tide of unbelief in the Inerrancy of the Bible and in the fact of the Resurrection of the Body of our Lord Jesus Christ, the outlook for our Missions abroad, and for our work at home, is appalling; hence this book.

The question of "Evolution" is also being largely discussed in our churches at the present day; just at this present moment possibly more than these other questions, but it has not been thought wise to treat this subject at any length in this book, for the question is not so fundamental and vital as the question of the Inerrancy and Authority of the Bible and the question of the Resurrection of Jesus Christ from the Dead.

INTRODUCTION

If we can settle these two questions, the question of Evolution will take care of itself. Furthermore, in the current discussions of Evolution, there is great confusion of thought both upon the part of the Conservatives and on the part of the Liberals. Neither side define with accuracy just what they mean by "Evolution," and the ardent advocates of Evolution, having given what they consider conclusive proof of the fact of an Evolution of a certain character, at once assert that they have proved the doctrine of Evolution in an entirely different sense. There is a similar confusion, though not so frequent or so gross, on the part of those who are contending against Evolution. No one should write either for or against Evolution without a careful definition of just what he means by Evolution. It is one of the most ambiguous words in common use today, and is used with a startling disregard for definiteness and accuracy by both sides in the present conflict. If someone more competent than the writer of this book does not take the subject up and handle it in an intelligent, clear, definite, thorough and satisfactory way, the writer may publish a book on the subject later, but he entertains the hope that a man whom he has in mind, or some other competent man, may do this work, and do it more thoroughly and satisfactorily than he himself could do it.

CONTENTS

CHAPTER		PAGE
I	Who Says, "The Bible is the Inerrant Word of God?"	13
II	Who Says, "The Bible is Not the Inerrant Word of God?"	33
III	Difficulties in the Bible: General Statements About Them	51
IV	Difficulties in the Bible: What Shall We Do With Them?	66
V	What to Do With the Bible	87
VI	Be Not Deceived: God Is Not Mocked	106
VII	Is It Absolutely Certain That the Body of Jesus That Was Nailed to the Cross, That Really Died, and That Was Laid in Joseph's Tomb, Was Raised from the Dead?	121
VIII	What One Gains by Believing in the Christ Who Rose from the Dead	167

IS THE BIBLE THE
INERRANT WORD OF GOD?

IS THE BIBLE THE INERRANT WORD OF GOD?

CHAPTER I

WHO SAYS, "THE BIBLE IS THE INERRANT WORD OF GOD"?

"For verily I say unto you, Till heaven and earth pass, one jot or one tittle shall in no wise pass from the law, till all be fulfilled."—Matt. 5:18.
"The scripture cannot be broken."—Jno. 10:35.
"Making the word of God of none effect through your tradition."—Mark 7:13.

The Question, Is the Bible the Inerrant Word of God? is the most fundamental of all questions in Religion or Ethics. If the Bible is the Word of God, an absolutely reliable revelation from God Himself, regarding Himself, His nature, His character, His will, His purposes, His plans, and regarding man, his nature, his need, his ruin, the way of his redemption, his duty and his destiny, then we have a sure starting point from which we can proceed to the conquest of the entire domain of Religious and Ethical truth. But if the Bible is not the Inerrant Word of God, if it is only the result of man's thinking, speculating and guessing regarding the great themes with which it has

Is the Bible the Inerrant Word of God?

to do, and therefore not at all dependable, even though it be the best result of man's thinking, speculating and guessing in existence, we are all at sea, drifting we know not whither, though we may be perfectly sure that we are not drifting toward any safe port. It is at this point that the great battle is to be fought out. Here should be the great line of cleavage and separation in the professing church today. The old distinctions between Presbyterians and Methodists, between Baptists and Congregationalists, between Lutherans and Episcopalians, have largely lost their significance for most of us. They have lost all of their significance for me. To be more exact, they never had any great significance for me. I am a Presbyterian because I believe a man ought to belong to and be responsible to some definite body of believers. I do not believe in guerrilla warfare. But I would not go across the road to make any other man a Presbyterian, but I would go a long ways and work hard to convince any man that this dear old Book, to which I owe everything I am and everything I may have ever accomplished in the world, is the absolutely dependable Word of God. I have far more fellowship with and joy in a Baptist who believes this Book to be the Inerrant Word of God, than I have with a Presbyterian who denies it or seeks to quibble about it and befog the issue, as some Presbyterians, I regret to say, do.

My subject then this morning is: *Who says, "The Bible is the Inerrant Word of God"?* By the Bible I do not mean any particular English Version of the Scriptures, the Authorized Version, the English Revision, or the American Standard Revision or any other Version, but the Scriptures as originally given. And we can now tell with substantial accuracy how the Scriptures as originally given, read. Furthermore, any of these versions mentioned are a substantially accurate rendition of the Hebrew and Aramaic of the original Old Testament manuscripts, and of the Greek of the original New Testament manuscripts, and to that extent they are "the Holy Scriptures," the Bible.

Let me repeat my subject: *Who says, "The Bible is the Inerrant Word of God"?* I have three texts: Matt. 5:18, "For verily I say unto you, Till heaven and earth pass, one jot or one tittle shall in no wise pass from the law, till all be fulfilled." Jno. 10:35, "The Scripture cannot be broken." Mark 7:13, "Making the word of God of none effect through your tradition."

We shall consider first Who says, the Bible is the Inerrant Word of God? and after that we shall consider, Who says, the Bible is not the Inerrant Word of God? Then you can judge for yourselves which group of witnesses you ought to believe. First, then, let us consider Who Says, "The Bible Is the Inerrant Word of God"?

1. In the first place, *our Lord Jesus Christ says so.* The attitude of Jesus Christ toward the Bible, toward both the Old Testament and the New Testament and His opinion in regard to the Bible as to whether its author was man or God is unmistakable.

(1) In one of our texts, Mark 7:13, *our Lord calls the Pentateuch "the Word of God" in so many words.*

His exact words are, "Making *the word of God* of none effect through your tradition, which ye have delivered." In the verses immediately preceding He has drawn a contrast between the teachings of the Pharisees and the Scribes on the one hand, and the teachings that Moses gave in the Pentateuch, not merely in the Ten Commandments but in other parts of the Pentateuch as well, on the other hand. And then He sums it all up by saying that they were "making *the word of God* of none effect through their tradition." In this way He calls the Pentateuch in so many words "the Word of God."

When I was holding meetings in England a high dignitary in the Church of England, a scholarly man, took exception to my calling the Bible "the Word of God," and in private correspondence said "the Bible nowhere claims to be "the Word of God." In reply I called his attention to this passage among others and showed him how our Lord Jesus Christ Himself called the Pentateuch "the Word of God."

(2) In another of my texts, Matt. 5:18, our Lord Jesus says: "For verily I say unto you, Till heaven and earth pass, *one jot or one tittle shall in no wise pass from the law,* till all be fulfilled." Now every Hebrew scholar knows that a "jot" was the Hebrew character Yedh (ʼ), the smallest character in the Hebrew alphabet, less than one half the size of any other character in the Hebrew alphabet, and that a "tittle" was simply the little horn that the Hebrews put on some of their letters, smaller than the cross we put on a *t*. So our Lord Jesus here sets the stamp of

Who Says, "The Bible is the Inerrant Word of God"?

His endorsement upon the absolute Inerrancy of the Law as originally given through Moses down to its smallest letter and smallest part of a letter. That is verbal inspiration with a vengeance.

Now of course these two passages refer primarily only to the Pentateuch. But if you can accept the Pentateuch you will not have much trouble with the rest of the Bible. This is the very part of the Bible where the hottest fight has always been waged between those who believe the Bible to be the Inerrant Word of God and those who think that much of it is only fable, or "folklore." Here is where you find the two accounts of Creation, about which so many superficial and ill-informed readers and teachers of the Bible gabble so much to their own satisfaction and so much to the disgust of all real students of the Bible. Here is where you have the story of the Fall, for which our "Modernists" and "New Theology Men," and "Eddyites" and "Theosophists" and "Spiritualists" and all that sort of folk have so much contempt, in which contempt they reveal their ignorance both of archaeological research and that type of present-day psychology that considers man as he really is and not as the dreamers would like him to be. Here is where we find the story of the Flood, of Sodom and Gomorrah and of Lot's wife (all of which were specifically endorsed as true history by our Lord). Here is where you find the story of the Manna, the miraculous opening of a path through the Red Sea, and the Smitten Rock that poured forth water, etc., etc., all things at which the destructive critics and their sympathizers most cavil. Is it not remarkable that our Lord Jesus, looking down the coming centuries and anticipating the discussions of this day in which you and I now live, should have set the seal of His endorsement in the most unmistakable and emphatic way on that very part of the Bible where the hottest battles are being waged today? That fact should make some of our self-sufficient critics of the Bible and of Jesus Christ, take pause and do some hard, serious, wholesome thinking.

(3) In another passage, Jno. 10:35, our Lord Jesus says, "The Scripture cannot be broken." He had just quoted a sentence from Psm. 82:6 as final authority and an end to all discussion in the matter in hand, and then He adds, "THE SCRIPTURES CANNOT BE BROKEN," thus setting the stamp of His endorsement to the absolute irrefragability or Inerrancy of the Old Testament Scriptures.

(4) In Luke 16:31, our Lord says, in recounting the story of the rich man and Lazarus, *"If they hear not Moses and the prophets, neither will they be persuaded, though one rose from the dead."* In these words He sets the seal of His endorsement upon both the Law of Moses, the Pentateuch, and upon the Prophets, which in the usage of His day included not merely the books we call Prophetical but many of the Historical books as well.

(5) In Luke 24:27, it is recorded of our Lord that, "beginning at *Moses and all the prophets,* he expounded unto *them in all the Scriptures* the things concerning himself." And in the forty-fourth verse of the same chapter He is recorded as saying, *"All things must be*

fulfilled, which were written in the law of Moses, and in the prophets, and in the Psalms." Now the Jew of our Lord's time divided his Bible, our present Old Testament Scriptures into three parts, "The Law of Moses," the Five Books that we call "The Pentateuch," "The Prophets," including not only most of the books that we call Prophetical but many of the Historical books as well, the material of which was derived from the "Prophets" and the "Psalms" or "Sacred Writings" including all the remaining books of our present Old Testament. And here our Lord Jesus Christ takes up each one of the three recognized divisions of the Old Testament and sets the stamp of His endorsement upon the Divine origin and Inerrancy of each and every one.

Putting these various utterances of our Lord together, we have His unqualified endorsement of the entire Old Testament as the Inerrant Word of God.

(6) But the Lord Jesus says that the books of the New Testament also are the Inerrant Word of God. It is true that not one book of the New Testament was yet written when our Lord was here on the earth, or when He left the earth as He ascended to the Father from Mount Olivet. But our Lord foresaw the writing of the books of the New Testament and unqualifiedly endorsed the books that were about to appear.

a. In Jno. 14:26, our Lord says, "But the Comforter, even the Holy Spirit, whom the Father will send in my name, *he* shall *teach you all things,* and *bring to your remembrance all that I said unto you."* In these words our Lord not only endorses the Apostolic teaching as being Divinely inspired, taught to them by the Holy Spirit, but He also endorsed their recollection of what He Himself had said. So that by our Lord's own word we have in the Apostolic records of the utterances *of Christ* not merely the Apostles' recollections of what Jesus Christ had said, but the Holy Spirit's recollection of what Jesus Christ had said. So the Apostolic records of the utterances of Jesus Christ can be absolutely depended upon.

b. Again in Jno. 16:12,13, our Lord says, "I have yet many things to say unto you, but ye cannot bear them now. Howbeit, when *He, the Spirit of truth,* is come, *He shall guide you into all the truth."* In these words our Lord sets the stamp of His endorsement upon the writings of the Apostles as not only being Divinely inspired, but as containing more truth than He Himself had given them (because they were not as yet ready to receive it), as indeed containing *"all the truth."*

To sum up what we have shown thus far: Jesus Christ says that the entire Old Testament and entire New Testament is the Inerrant Word of God. You cannot deny the Divine origin of this book, its Divine sufficiency and Inerrancy without discrediting Jesus Christ. Prove to me that this old book is not the Inerrant Word of God and I will give up Jesus Christ. As an honest, thinking man, as a man who carries out all things he believes to their logical issue, whatever that issue may be, I will have to give up Jesus Christ, if it is proven to me that the Bible is not the Inerrant Word of God. For Jesus Christ claimed to be a teacher sent from God who spoke the very words of God. He claimed this over and over again, and, if He was mistaken about the origin and the character of this book concerning which He has so much to say, He was a fraud, an unmitigated fraud. If these people are right who tell us that these incidents in the book of Genesis, for example, which our Lord has so plainly endorsed, are simply "folklore," or inaccurate and unreliable traditions of the day, then, beyond a question Jesus Christ was a fraud, an unmitigated fraud. But I begin at the other end of the argument, the logical end of the argument: I prove by undeniable facts that Jesus Christ was a teacher sent from God who spoke the very words of God, and therefore I am compelled to believe that the book which He endorsed as being the Inerrant Word of God is in reality such.

There are five unmistakably Divine testimonies that we can investigate for ourselves today without seeking light from these self-sufficient and greatly overrated "modern scholars" who talk very loudly and very pompously concerning matters about which they oftentimes know nothing, that Jesus Christ was what He claimed to be, a Teacher sent from God, Who spoke the very words of God. Jesus Christ is accredited to us by the Divine life that He lived; for He lived as never man lived. He is accredited to us by the Divine words that He spoke; for He spoke as no man ever spoke. He is accredited to us by the Divine works that He wrought; for He wrought as never man wrought, not merely healing the sick, which others have done, but cleansing the leper by His mere word, stilling the tempest and the raging of the sea by His mere word, raising the dead by His mere word, turning water into wine and feeding the five thousand people with five loaves and two small fishes, which were creative acts. He is also accredited to us by His Divine influence upon all subsequent history. He is accredited to us by His resurrection from the dead, the best proven fact of history, which is the Lord God Almighty's stamp of endorsement on Jesus Christ's claims. Therefore I am compelled, compelled by the inexorable logic of conclusively proven facts to accept the authority of Jesus Christ as a teacher sent from God, Who spoke the very words of God. Consequently I am compelled to accept the entire book which He endorsed as being the Inerrant Word of God, as being in reality such. There may be difficulties with individual passages in the Bible that I in my very limited knowledge cannot explain. But a man is not a philosopher but a fool who gives up a thoroughly established theorem because there are difficulties that he cannot explain. No reputable scientist in any department of science ever does that. The proof that Jesus is a teacher sent from God who spoke the very words of God is absolutely conclusive, indeed it is overwhelming, and therefore I unquestioningly accept *His* say-so, however difficult it may be to reconcile with some things I seem to know. Therefore, when the Lord Jesus says, as he continually does say, that this Book is the Inerrant "Word of God" I heartily believe it, I would be an egregious fool if I did not.

2. In the second place, *History says that, the Bible*

Who Says, "The Bible is the Inerrant Word of God"?

is the Inerrant Word of God. One of the voices to which all really wise men listen is the voice of history, and the voice of history is very clear in its pronouncement that the Bible is the Word of God. In numerous ways history proclaims the Bible to be the Word of God. I will mention only three.

(1) In the first place, *the voice of history proclaims the Bible to be the Word of God by the uniform outcome of all the attempts that have been made through eighteen centuries to discredit and destroy the Bible.* It is so self-evident as to be practically axiomatic that what man has produced man can destroy. If then men produced the Bible why have eighteen centuries of assault upon the Bible been unable to destroy it? The Bible was scarcely born before the Bible was intensely hated. Men had too much of the Devil in them to do anything but hate a book that was so full of God, from its first word to its last, a book that begins with the words, "In the beginning God," and closes with the words, "the grace of the Lord Jesus be with the saints," and that reveals God by plain statement or by clear implication on every page. The devilish hate in the human heart against this Divine Book has been most active, most aggressive, most persistent, most relentless. As the Devil sought through a human king to destroy the Son of God in His infancy, he also tried to destroy the Word of God in its infancy through kings in the world of thought. The Bible has been attacked by many men of great ability and power, with all the intellectual, scientific, philosophical, political and physical forces they could command. First of all

Fronto, probably the greatest rhetorician and teacher of eloquence of his day, the man chosen by the great emperor of Rome, Antoninus Pius, to have charge of the education of his more illustrious son, Marcus Aurelius Antoninus, attacked the Bible with all the powers of his brilliant mind and gifted pen. He was determined to discredit and destroy it, but he failed utterly. Then Celsus, a man of such learning and ability that most of our modern infidels from Tom Paine to Robert Ingersoll, and also the reputed "scholars" of "the *modern* critical school," have for the most part simply echoed and embellished the arguments of this bitter enemy of Christ of the second century, assaulted the Bible not only with literary attacks but by stirring up persecution against those who believed in it, and with every resource at his command attempted to discredit and destroy the Bible. He so utterly failed that he recognized his failure and tried to win by compromise where he had failed in direct assault. Porphyry, the recognized leader of the Neo-Platonic philosophers of his day, tried it with all the depth and subtilty of his philosophy, and he also utterly failed. Lucian, one of the first and most gifted satirists of all literary history, tried to discredit the Bible, seeking to destroy it by the keen shafts of his satire; but he failed. Diocletian, who had at his command all the military, political, and financial resources of the mightiest empire the world has ever known, Rome at the zenith of its glory and might, brought every force at his disposal to bear against the Bible with the relentless determination to discredit and destroy it. He issued an edict that every Bible in the Roman Empire should be destroyed. That failed. He then issued a sterner edict that every one who possessed a Bible should be put to death, but that failed. So man's determined efforts to destroy the Bible have gone on for eighteen long centuries. Every instrument of destruction that human wisdom, human learning, human science, human philosophy, human satire, human cunning, human force and human brutality, could bring to bear against a book, has been brought to bear against this Book. With what result? That the Bible has a firmer hold upon the confidence and affections of the wisest and best men and women in the world than it ever had before. The Bible will not be destroyed, men cannot destroy it, that is historically demonstrated, and therefore it is historically demonstrated that man never produced it. The testimony of history for eighteen centuries is uniform and bears indisputable witness to the fact that the Bible is indestructible by all the forces that man can bring to bear against it, and that therefore as we have just said man never produced it, and that therefore the Bible is beyond honest question not of human origin, but *is the Word of God.* Man-made philosophies have failed and passed away, man-made scientific systems have failed and passed away, man-made governments have failed and passed away, man-made kingdoms have failed and passed away, man-made empires have failed and passed away, man-made civilizations have failed and passed away, man-made literature has failed and passed away, the God-made Bible has never failed throughout all the centuries of its existence. It still stands. "Heaven and earth shall pass away, but God's Word," this immortal, imperishable Old Book "shall never pass away" (Matt. 24:35).

(2) In the second place, *History proclaims the Bible to be the Word of God by fulfilling its prophecies, fulfilling them exactly, and minutely.* The Bible, both the Old Testament and the New Testament, is very largely taken up with predictions. The destructive critics are fond of saying that, "There is no predictive element in Bible prophecy." That is one of the fundamental postulates of their whole system. But no intelligent person can maintain that except by deliberately closing his eyes to facts so manifest that even an intelligent child must see them or else by the most extravagant and ridiculous distortion of plain facts. Predictions about the Israelitish people, predictions about individuals, about Abraham and his descendants and about David, for example, predictions about many Gentile cities and nations, Babylon, Nineveh, Tyre, the Egyptians, Grecians, Romans and others, predictions most minute and particular about the coming King of Israel, the Messiah the Christ, have been fulfilled to the letter centuries after they were made *and they are still being fulfilled right before our eyes today.* Now any book that has the power of looking centuries into the future and predicting with minuteness and precision and accuracy of time, person, place and circumstance, events to occur centuries later, must have for its author the only Being in the universe Who knows the end from the beginning, that is God, and history demonstrates that the Bible has this power. The history of the

first century, the history of the second century, the history of the third century, the history of the fourth century, the history of the seventeenth and the eighteenth and nineteenth centuries and the history of the twentieth century proclaim with one united voice, to which only the consummate fool will turn a deaf ear, "The Bible is the Word of God."

(3) In the third place, *History proclaims the Bible to be the Word of God by exhibiting before the eyes of us all the Divine Power this Book has had, as an absolutely certain historical fact, in the lives of individuals and in the history of nations.* This Book, as an indisputable fact of history, has done for individuals and nations what no other book nor all other books put together have ever done, what only a Divine Book, *i.e.*, a book that came from God, could do. It admits of no honest question that there is in this Book a power, to transform, gladden, beautify, an ennoble human lives, a power to lift men up to God that no other book possesses and that all other books taken together do not possess. Even so stubborn a scientific skeptic as Thomas Huxley admitted the peerless power of this Book. It is one of the most confidently believed axioms of twentieth century physical science, that a stream can rise no higher than its source, and I submit that a book that has a power to lift men up to God that no other book possesses must have come down from God in a way that no other book has. There is no answer to this argument, and so history proclaims with unwavering and clear, ringing, trumpet voice, "This Book is God's Word."

And history declares that there is a power in this Book that no other book possess and all other books taken together do not possess to lift up communities and nations as well as to lift up individuals. What were recognized as the three greatest nations of the earth a little over seven years ago? England, the United States and Germany. But to what did these three greatest nations of the earth owe all that was best in their individual life, in their domestic life, in their social life, in their business life, in their political life? Beyond a question to the Bible. And then the fatal hour came: one of these nations gave up its faith in the Bible. Nietzsche, Häckel, Wellhausen, Graf, and other infidel or destructively critical scholars ruled the thought of their universities, their literary men, their political leaders and through them of most of the people; and today the civilization, the culture, the social life, the home life, the business of Germany, once so great, lies in a tangled mass of apparently hopeless wreck and ruin. The Bible of Luther saved Germany and made her great in the eyes of God and man. The Bible of Wellhausen and Graf and such-like "scholars" have damned Germany and made her a laughingstock before men and demons. And Professor Kent with his "Shorter Bible," aided and abetted oftentimes by Y.M.C.A. and Y.W.C.A. secretaries all over the land and across the seas in China, and by quite a notable part of self-proclaimed "scholars" in many theological seminaries and universities in both England and America are trying to get us to give up the Bible that has made us great and accept the bible of the higher critics, "The

Shorter Bible," the bible that wrecked Germany. Will we do it? Not for one moment unless we are hopeless idiots and totally unmoved by the clear voice of history, to say nothing of the voice of the Lord Jesus, the Glorious Son of God, Who spoke the very words of God.

3. Our subject is: Who Says, The Bible is the Inerrant Word of God? We have seen that Jesus Christ says so. We have seen that the voice of eighteen centuries of history says so. In the third place: *All of the men and women who live nearest God and know God best say so.* Some great scholars may deny that the Bible is the Inerrant Word of God: no great saint denies it. What do I mean by "saint"? I mean the man who is wholly God's, the man who has separated himself unto God, the man who has renounced utterly his own will and unreservedly submitted to God's will, whatever it may be, and surrendered his own thinking and accepted God's thinking, and given his mind over unreservedly to God for God to teach him as He will, the man who has put his life and whole being at God's disposal for God to send him where He will, use him as He will, do with him as He will, the man who lives near God and deeply knows God. Show me a man who has done this and who after he has done it has deeply pondered this Book so that he is competent to judge whether this Book is God's book or not, and I will show you every time a man who has a fixed and unshakable faith that this Book from its first verse to its last verse is God's Inerrant Word. I challenge you to produce me one

single exception. I have thrown out substantially the same challenge literally around this globe, and it has never been taken up. It is still open.

With absolute unanimity all the men and women of all lands who live nearest God and know God best say this Book is His Book, and I opine that their opinion is best worth accepting. Do not you think so? We have already seen that the Lord Jesus says so, and of course of all the men and women who have ever walked this earth He lived nearest God and knew God best.

4. We have seen that Jesus Christ says that the Bible is the Inerrant Word of God, we have seen that the voice of history of all the centuries of the Bible's existence, says so, and we have seen that all the men and women who live nearest God and know God best say that the Bible is the Inerrant Word of God, but there is still One other who says so too. *The Holy Spirit says so.* The Holy Spirit, who lives and speaks today is ready to declare it distinctly to the soul of every man and woman here who puts himself in such a relation to God and to His living Spirit, through Whom God speaks to men today, that the Holy Spirit can speak to Him. Our Lord Jesus says in Jno. 8:47, "He that is of God (literally, out of God, *i.e.*, born of God), heareth the words of God." That is to say that every one who has been born of God is taught by the Spirit of God and therefore recognizes God's words when he hears them and listens to them, and every one so born of God recognizes in the words of this Book the voice of that God of whom he is born. Again our Lord Jesus says in

Who Says, "The Bible is the Inerrant Word of God"?

Jno. 10:27, "My sheep hear my voice," by which He evidently means that every one who has become His sheep gets an instinct by which he knows the true Shepherd's Voice from every other voice and he knows that the voice which talks to him from this Book is the voice of the True Shepherd. Now here is a test that each one of us can apply for himself and thus find out for himself whether what our Lord Jesus says is true or not. That is one of the great and unique characteristics of the Bible, it offers tests by which anyone can try it and find out for himself independently of priest, preacher or scholar whether its claims are true or not. The simplest statement and complete summing up of these tests is found in our Lord's own words in Jno. 7:17, "If any man *willeth to do his will, he* shall know of the teaching, whether it be of God, or whether I speak from myself." Try it for yourself. I have personally known hundreds, yes thousands, who have tried it and it has never failed. Before visiting a well known university center in England, one of the most prominent men in one of the colleges composing that university had openly denied in his classes the infallibility of Jesus Christ either in doctrine or in conduct. After my meetings this same scholar presided at an Evangelical Missionary meeting and announced his acceptance of the truth that he had formerly denied, and he was kind enough to say, "Under God I owe all this to Dr. Torrey." This was a notable instance but only one among many. Ordinary men have tried it. I sometimes wish I had kept and collated and classified all the letters I have received and testimonies that have been given me by former skeptics, infidels, Unitarians, destructive critics, agnostics and atheists, of all classes of society from day laborers up to brilliant university professors, eminent lawyers and judges, who have put this matter to the test and met the conditions and the living Spirit of God, not a Spirit who only lived and spoke in former days, spoke to and through the Apostles, but Who lives and speaks directly to men to-day, has spoken directly to them testifying that this Book is the very Word of God.

To sum up, our Lord Jesus says that the Bible is the Inerrant Word of God, the history of eighteen centuries has proclaimed the Bible to be the Inerrant Word of God, all the men and women who live nearest God and know God best unhesitatingly declare that the Bible is the Inerrant Word of God, the Holy Spirit declares to the individual soul that puts himself in such an attitude that the Holy Spirit can speak to him, that the Bible is the Inerrant Word of God. Is the Bible then the Inerrant Word of God or is it not? Beyond the shadow of a doubt, it is.

CHAPTER II

WHO SAYS, "THE BIBLE IS NOT THE INERRANT WORD OF GOD"?

"God hath said, ye shall not eat of it, neither shall ye touch it, lest ye die. And the serpent said unto the woman, ye shall not surely die."—Gen. 3: 3, 4.

My subject this morning is: *"Who Says, "The Bible is not the Inerrant Word of God"?* You will find my text in Gen. 3:3, 4: *"God* hath *said,* ye shall not eat of it, neither shall ye touch it, lest ye die. And *the serpent said* unto the woman, ye shall not surely die."

Last Sunday morning we considered the question, Who says, "The Bible is the Inerrant Word of God"? We saw that our Lord Jesus Christ says so, that the voice of history says so, that the voice of history proclaims the Bible to be the Inerrant Word of God in three ways: First, by the uniform outcome of all the attempts that have been made through eighteen centuries to discredit and destroy the Bible; second, by fulfilling its prophecies, fulfilling them exactly and minutely; third, by exhibiting before the eyes of us all the Divine Power this Book has had, as an absolutely certain fact of history, in the lives of individuals and in the history of nations. Next, we saw that all the men

Is the Bible the Inerrant Word of God?

and women who live nearest God and know God best, say that the Bible *is* the Inerrant Word of God; and finally, we know that the Holy Spirit, Who lives and speaks to men today, also says so.

Now, this morning, let us frankly and honestly and fairly and fully look at the other side, and see who they are who say, "The Bible is *not* the Inerrant Word of God." So, my subject this morning is the exact counterpart of my subject last Sunday morning. My subject last Sunday morning was: Who says, "The Bible *is* the Inerrant Word of God"? My subject this morning is: Who says, "The Bible is *not* the Inerrant Word of God"?

There are many in this day in which we are living who say so. Just who are they? There are six classes of persons who say, "The Bible is not the Inerrant Word of God."

I. The Vilest Elements of Society Say that the Bible is not the Inerrant Word of God

First of all, then, *the vilest elements of society say so.* We shall see directly that they are not by any means the only class that say so, but they constitute one large class who say so. Let me repeat it: the vilest elements of society say that the Bible is not the Inerrant Word of God. Go to the slums of any city, and among the drunkards, the prostitutes, the thieves, the gunmen, the anarchists, the Bolshevists, and the men and women in general who contend against law and order and good government, and moral decency, you will find plenty of men and women, men and women, oftentimes, of gifted minds and fine culture, but who have gone down through lust or drink or some other form of sin, who ridicule the idea of the Bible being the Inerrant Word of God. They have the arguments, or the jeers, of Tom Paine and Robert Ingersoll, and, also, of the so-called "Modern School of Critics," at their tongue's end.

I met, one morning, in a store in Minneapolis, a man of fine education and brilliant mind, but who had gone down through drink, gone so far down that from being the most brilliant lawyer in that part of the world he had reached almost the bottom. I approached him and began to speak to him about his moral and spiritual condition. He was partially intoxicated at the time. In reply to my words, he said, "Torrey, I don't like you; you are too narrow." "Now," he continued, "See here. Honor bright, what do you think would become of me if I should drop dead right here now?" I replied, "John, you would go straight to hell, and you would deserve to." "What have I done?" he asked. I replied, "I will tell you what you have done. You have got your wife's heart right under your heel, and are grinding the very life out of it, and what is worse than that, you are trampling under foot the Son of God." "Ah!" he said, with a laugh, "You are too narrow. I believe in the New Theology," and then he began to mention some of the leading teachers in a prominent theological seminary that had gone astray from the truth. A little later still, when he had sunk still lower, I met him on Washington Avenue near

Third Avenue South. He was the very picture of wretchedness and ruin. I stopped him again and began to talk to him. He listened, for he was beginning to get thoroughly tired of the wreck and ruin that had come into his life and into his home through sin, but when I pressed upon him an immediate acceptance of Christ, he replied, "I do not believe in your Christ, and I do not believe in your Bible. I am an agnostic." I answered, "It does not make a particle of difference, John, what you believe. If you accept the Lord Jesus Christ, He will save you; if you reject Him, you are a lost man." He turned and went down the street with a hollow laugh, a very bitter laugh. He sank deeper and deeper, bolstered up in his ruinous course by his denial that the Bible was the Inerrant Word of God. He became a tramp in the City of New York, and then he came to his senses and threw to the winds his agnosticism and his denial that the Bible was the Word of God, and accepted the Bible as the Word of God and Jesus Christ as the Son of God and his own Divine Savior, and was lifted by the power of that book and of the Christ of that book out of his utter ruin to become one of the most honored men in the whole country.

Of course, you can find in the purlieus of our cities some of the wrecks of society who have not lost all traces of the faith in which godly fathers and mothers instructed them in their innocent childhood, and who, because of this fact, are won back to God and to noble lives, but "the slums" of society is one of the places where infidelity in all its forms, the substantial denial

Who Says, "The Bible is Not the Inerrant Word of God"?

that the Bible is the Inerrant Word of God, most thrives.

You can go out among the wild and lawless in the deserts and mountains, and you will find among them plenty of men and women who say with most confident and most vehement assurance, "The Bible is not the Inerrant Word of God." A friend of mine, in the mountains of West Virginia, was driven by a storm to seek refuge in a lonely hut, late at night. This friend, to her dismay, found that the hut was inhabited by a desperate old woman, who made most of her living by selling bootleg whisky across the river, near at hand. She was one of the most prominent members of the notorious McCoy gang. The female outlaw gave her shelter for the night. My friend asked for something to read and this desperate old woman brought out a book in which she kept the family record of births and deaths, such as Christians kept in the olden days in the family Bible. What do you think the book was?—Ingersoll's "Mistakes of Moses," from which, along with its progenitor, Tom Paine's "Age of Reason," "the modern critical school" have borrowed so copiously. That was her Bible.

In my first pastorate, I lived, for a time, in the home of a man who professed to be an infidel, and he was a very decent man in many ways. An infidel lecturer came to town, and I went to hear what he had to say, and this respectable infidel went also. When I looked around and saw the character of the crew that was gathered to hear this man, who, with quite a little ability, retailed the cheap jokes of Robert Ingersoll and Tom Paine, I did not feel quite in my element. When we got home, I said to my infidel friend, "How did you enjoy the lecture?" He replied, "I did not like the kind of crowd that was there." I replied, "That is the kind of a crowd your view of the Bible creates." And it is so.

Go to the publishers of obscene literature and the manufacturers of instruments for all kinds of illicit and indecent purposes and you will find plenty of men and women who deny that the Bible is the Inerrant Word of God. Indeed, the publishers of obscene literature in the United States had Colonel Robert Ingersoll as their attorney when they were resisting the Government's attempts to suppress their nefarious, disgusting and outrageous business. Colonel Robert Ingersoll was their idol. In England, also, two of the ablest and, in some ways, most decent leaders of infidelity, whom I shall not name, one a man and the other a woman, were both incarcerated for publishing an indecent book and promulgating, for the practice of married and unmarried women, a disgusting and illegal way of preventing the conception of children. Yes, the vilest elements of society say that, "The Bible is not the Inerrant Word of God." We shall see, directly, that far more respectable and reputable elements of society say so too. But we must consider the subject both honestly and fully and it is well to always bear in mind the fact that this class of society says, "The Bible is not the Inerrant Word of God; that just as all the men and women who live nearest God, and know God best, are the most positive in their assertions that "the Bible is the Inerrant Word of God," so, also, the men and women who live farthest from God, and who know God least, are the ones who are the most positive in their assertion that, "the Bible is not the Inerrant Word of God."

II. Men Who Are Puffed Up in Their Fleshly Mind

In the second place, *men who are puffed up in their fleshly mind, because of a small measure of intellectual superiority in scientific or philosophical lines to the average man, say that "The Bible is not the Inerrant Word of God."* I do not wish you to think, for one moment, that I maintain that it is only the vilest and most dangerous elements of society who deny that "the Bible is the Inerrant Word of God." No, not at all. I began with them because I wished to begin at the bottom and lead up to those who are higher and better, and lead you on to the very best, before I ask you to decide between the two classes of witnesses—those who say, "The Bible is the Inerrant Word of God," and those who say, "The Bible is not the Inerrant Word of God."

There are men and women who have a measure of intellectual superiority, usually, it is true, a rather small measure of superiority, in scientific or philosophic attainments above the average man or woman, and who have become puffed up because of the consciousness of this superiority, and love to pose as "the Scholarly Class," as if they had a monopoly on all the scholarship there is in the world today, and forget or deliberately ignore the fact that the really great Semitic scholars, as, for example, Professor Robert Dick Wilson, of Princeton, and Professor David Samuel Margoliouth, of Oxford University, England, and almost all the great archaeologists who have done actual, original field work, are definitely arrayed on the conservative side—I say, there is this class of studious men, of no mean intellectual caliber, who say that, "the Bible is not the Inerrant Word of God." And they are cocksure that it is not, and they have a very supercilious contempt, or, at least, a great patronizing pity, for the preachers and other people, whom they characterize as "Reactionaries," or "Obscurantists," or "Mediaeval," or "Archaic" or "Antediluvian," who still hold to the belief that "the Bible is the Inerrant Word of God." The fundamental trouble with these men is set forth by God Himself in a remarkable sentence in Rom. 1:22, "Professing themselves to be wise, they became fools." Of course, I mention no names, most of you can supply numerous names for yourselves.

III. Men of Real Ability in Other Lines of Thought, but Who Have Not Given the Bible the Special Thought and Thorough Attention and Careful Study that Is Demanded to Make One an Authority in That Special Line

There is a third class who say that "The Bible is not the Inerrant Word of God," men of real and unusual ability in other lines of thought, but who have

Who Says, "The Bible is Not the Inerrant Word of God"?

not given the Bible the special thought and thorough attention and careful study that is demanded to make one an authority in that particular line. There are many men whose real and rare ability in the lines in which they specialize, and in which they justly shine as leaders, and whose authority *in their own line* we gladly acknowledge, but who have given to the Bible very little of that special thought, and thoroughgoing attention, and careful and complete study, that is necessary to give anyone's opinion any great weight in any line of research, who hold very tenaciously to their opinion, and are very outspoken in their declaration of their opinion, that "the Bible is not the Inerrant Word of God." But the fact that a man is a master thinker in Astronomy does not necessarily make his opinion of any great value along geological lines. The fact that a man is the most advanced and greatest thinker in the world in the domain of Chemistry does not make his opinion of any great value in questions of Civics and Political Economy. The fact that a man knows more about Constitutional Law than any other man now living, does not make his opinion of as much value in the field of Therapeutics as that of an obscure country doctor. And the fact that a man is a great thinker in the domain of Physical Science or Metaphysical Philosophy does not, necessarily, give his opinion any great weight in the field of Theology or Biblical Criticism. I take off my hat to Thomas Edison in questions about electricity, but when it comes to God, or the Bible, I know a multitude of Sunday-School boys and girls whose opinion is of more value than his. When it comes to the matter of designing and manufacturing weapons to slaughter our fellowmen in ruthless war, I acknowledge the authority of Hiram Maxim; but when it comes to questions about Ethics and God and the Bible, I would prefer the opinions of someone who knows something concerning what he is talking about. It is both amazing and ludicrous the way in which the enemies of the Bible call in as expert witnesses men who have never given any attention whatever to that line of study. They do it in no other branch of study in the world. They would be considered fools if they did. But they do it constantly, when it comes to questions about God and the Bible. This method is thoroughly unscientific, illogical, and irrational. No one ever thought of seeking Charles Darwin's opinion about music. One of the most pathetic incidents in his life was when Ole Bull wished to play the violin for him. The old man (with tears, if I remember correctly) acknowledged that he had allowed that part of his natural make-up to become atrophied by disuse. But Darwin has constantly been cited as an authority in religion, a subject about which, alas! he knew very little, and, therefore, his opinion about the Bible is of less value than that of a negro washerwoman, who has taken the time and made the sacrifices necessary to get acquainted with God.

IV. Men and Women Who Do Not Think for Themselves, But Accept, Without Careful Investigation, Whatever Is Called "Scholarly"

There is a fourth class of men and women who say that, "the Bible is not the Inerrant Word of God," men and women who do not think for themselves, but simply accept with avidity and without question or careful investigation, whatever is dubbed "scholarly." Some people in bygone days were frightened by the word, "orthodox"! Far more, in these days, are frightened by the word, "scholarly." Many a twentieth-century preacher would rather sacrifice the sacred convictions of his parents, and of his own pure and earnest and consecrated young manhood, than have anyone whisper that he was not "scholarly," or "up to date," or "modern," or "abreast of the times." *The word "scholarly" is a twentieth-century bug-a-boo to frighten fools with, and it is frightening a lot of them.* Tell some men that such and such a view of the Bible presents "the consensus of opinion of the most advanced scholars," and they will swallow it as eagerly as a bull-head will swallow bait, hook and sinker. A very large proportion of the seemingly intelligent people, preachers, college professors, and high school teachers, and Y. W. C. A. secretaries, who deny that the Bible is the Inerrant Word of God, belong to this class. These people are by no means fools or illiterate, but they are not real students, or careful thinkers. They do not think; they simply gorge, and they have been fed up on the wrong kind of provender. They have been told that "all scholars agree," and that settles it for them. They take it for granted that the statement is true, and as they eagerly desire to be numbered with the "scholars," they say so, too. They are merely echoes, and, unfortunately, they echo the wrong voices. There are in these days a vast host of half educated, or rather, half instructed people who fancy that it is a mark of advanced scholarship to be a theological "Liberal," or "Modernist," and so they join that party. It is much easier to get a reputation for scholarship that way, than by doing the hard work and the hard thinking that are necessary to become a real scholar, and so they adopt that plan, and this sort of Brummagem scholarship goes as well with the mass of men as the real article.

Some years ago, there was in the South a young Methodist Episcopal preacher. He was not altogether without brains, but he had had little education. He had some education, he had gone as far as the Sophomore year in a special course in one of the Georgia Colleges; and yet this half-baked "theologian" undertook to criticize the Bishop, who had been President of the very College where he had gone as far as the Sophomore year *in a special Course*. The Bishop was a scholar, and he was a Bible scholar. He carried the Hebrew Bible with him wherever he went, and studied it constantly. He was also a conservative. But this professedly "scholarly," but really very meagerly educated, preacher said, "Oh! you know the Bishop is no scholar." That sort of thing is common. A woman of this type has recently been teaching a class of teachers of the various Sunday-Schools of one of our suburbs, and, with a very superior air, has been airing her ignorance about the supposedly contradictory accounts of creation in the first and second chapters of Genesis. The woods are full of them. And many of our Sunday-Schools and Churches are submitting to that sort of mischievous and soul-destroying nonsense without a protest.

V. Men Who Have the Purely Intellectual Equipment, the Mental Vigor and Grasp, and the Technical Knowledge of the Languages in Which the Bible Was Originally Written, to Be Intelligent Bible Students and Who Really Have Studied the Bible Minutely and Carefully and Profoundly, But Who Lack the Spiritual Insight That Is Necessary to Make Their Estimates of a Preëminently Spiritual Book of Any Real Value

There is a fifth class, a class of far higher order than any I have mentioned so far, who also say that, "The Bible is not the Inerrant Word of God," viz., Men who have the purely intellectual equipment, the mental vigor and grasp, and the technical knowledge of the languages in which the Bible was originally written, to fit them to be intelligent Bible students and who really have studied the Bible minutely and carefully and profoundly, but who lack the spiritual insight that is necessary to make their estimates of a preeminently spiritual book of any real value. It needs no argument to prove that it takes spiritual discernment to qualify one to be an authoritative judge regarding a spiritual book. Paul certainly had common sense on his side, as well as the Divine inspiration to which he lays claim in the immediate context, when he said in 1 Cor. 2:14, "Now the natural man receiveth not the things of the Spirit of God: for they are foolishness unto him; and he cannot know them, because they are spiritually judged." A thorough knowledge of Greek, and of Hebrew, and of Aramaic, and of the cognate languages, no more qualifies a man to be a competent judge of the authorship of the Bible, because the Bible was written in these languages, than a thorough knowledge of paints qualifies one to be a competent critic of art. To be that, a man needs esthetic sense, and to be able to judge the Bible, a man needs spiritual sense. I would as soon expect a man to appreciate the Sistine Madonna because he was not color blind, as to expect an unspiritual man to understand and appreciate the Bible simply because he understands the laws of the grammar and the vocabulary of the languages in which the Bible was written. I would as soon think of setting a man to teach Art merely because he understood paints, as to set him to teach the Bible merely because he understood Greek and Hebrew and Aramaic. Here is where the Church of Jesus Christ is making today not only a stupendous blunder, but an almost incredible blunder. It is filling its theological Seminaries with teachers of bright minds and of abundant scholarship, of a certain sort, but without the clearness of spiritual vision that comes from an intelligent, deliberate, unreserved surrender of their will to God, and from a realization of the utter insufficiency and worthlessness in the things of God of our own natural wisdom, and of the need that they themselves be taught by the living Spirit of God, before they are competent to teach others, who are to become ministers of the Gospel. No wonder that some of our theological Seminaries have become cemeteries —graveyards of spiritual life, and also volcanoes that are belching forth the confusing and smothering smoke and gas and destroying hot lava of a host of practical infidels.to corrupt the life and doctrine of the Church, and to destroy its spiritual fertility.

VI. The Men Who Were Directly Responsible for the Awful War that Has Recently Ended

There is a sixth class of men and women who say that, "The Bible is not the Inerrant Word of God," viz., the men who were responsible for the awful world war, from which we are just emerging. This awful war, with its staggering cost in money and men, with its wrecked homes and ruined characters, its shipwreck of nations, and its aftermath of hatred, immorality, violence, murder, anarchy, personal and social madness, world-wide bankruptcy, starvation, gloom, and general social and political and international damnation, is directly due to the teaching of destructive criticism in German Universities. The destructive criticism of Graf, Wellhausen, and their compeers, which so many professors in Theological Seminaries, and so many writers on theological themes, are trying so hard to force upon our pulpits and our pews, upon our preachers, our Sunday-School teachers, and even young Sunday-School scholars, by a thoroughly and skillfully organized propaganda, not only at home, but in China and other foreign fields—this destructive criticism was responsible for the great war. It undermined the faith of the German people in the authority of the Book of God. It got them to substitute "the good old German God of War" for the God of this Book, and thus made possible the most damnable war in all history. When I was a student in the University of Leipzig, one night, in a meeting which some of us American students had weekly with Professor Franz Delitzsch, one of us asked him how we should present these views to the people. He looked at the questioner with amazement, almost indignation, "Present them to the people?" he exclaimed, "They are none of the people's business. They are only for scholars." We assured him that even if that would work in Germany, it would not work in America, but that what scholars knew now, the people would soon know. And it did not work even in Germany. The people got to know the practical infidelity that there was in the hearts of many of their preachers, and German faith in the Bible as the Inerrant Word of God went by the board, and the infidelity of Graf, Wellhausen & Company took its place, and the war came as a logical consequence.

Professor Shailer Matthews of Chicago University, in his just indignation against the awful war, and in his clear discernment that that war was the legitimate child of present-day German Philosophy, speaking in this city, and I think in this building, at a National gathering of Teachers and Educators of America not many years ago, demanded that we give up, and shut out of our educational institutions in America, the German Philosophy that was responsible for this war. But this same Professor Shailer Mathews, as I pointed out at the time, is himself one of the persons most responsible here in these United States for trying to force the very worst feature of German Philosophy and thinking, its philosophy and thinking regarding the Bible, upon our Theological Seminaries, our Universities, our Colleges, our High Schools, and even upon our Sunday-Schools.

Such are the men who say that "the Bible is not the Inerrant Word of God." I will not stop to sum up in detail who they are, but will simply say that if you will stop to think, you will see that there is not one among them whose opinion on a subject like this is worth ten cents.

Here, then, the case stands, awaiting your verdict. On the one side, we have our Lord Jesus Christ saying that "the Bible is the Inerrant Word of God," and we have eighteen centuries of history proclaiming that the Bible *is* the Inerrant Word of God, and we have all the men and women who live nearest God, and know God best, declaring that, "the Bible is the Inerrant Word of God," and we have the Holy Spirit, Who lives today, crying with no uncertain voice in our individual hearts, "the Bible is the Inerrant Word of God." And on the other hand, you have only the six classes I have described, not one of them possessing any well-grounded authority in such a matter, declaring that "The Bible is not the Inerrant Word fo God." Which will you believe? It is up to you. Decide for yourselves. I know how you will decide, for I am addressing, for the most part, intelligent and honest-minded men and women, who really wish to know and obey the truth.

Oh, blessed Book of God! Whose every statement is to be believed, whose every promise is to be trusted, whose every warning is to be heeded, whose every commandment to be obeyed, and whose every privilege, for time and eternity, is to be appropriated.

CHAPTER III

DIFFICULTIES IN THE BIBLE—GENERAL STATEMENTS ABOUT THEM

"Our beloved Brother Paul also, according to the wisdom given to him, wrote unto you; as also in all his epistles, speaking in them of these things; *wherein are some things hard to be understood,* which the ignorant and unsteadfast wrest, as they do also the other scriptures, unto their own destruction."

Our subject this morning is: *"Difficulties in the Bible."* You will find the text in 2 Pet. 3:15, 16: "Our beloved brother Paul also, according to the wisdom given to him, wrote unto you; as also in all his epistles, speaking in them of these things; *wherein are some things hard to be understood,* which the ignorant and unsteadfast wrest, as they do also the other scriptures, unto their own destruction."

Two weeks ago this morning we considered the question: "Who says, the Bible is the Inerrant Word of God?" We saw that our Lord Jesus Christ said so, that the voice of history says so, that all the men and women who live nearest God and know God best, say so, and that the Holy Spirit, who lives today and speaks to men today, also says so. A week ago this morning we considered the subject, "Who says that the Bible is *not* the Inerrant Word of God?" and we saw that there were six classes of people who deny that the Bible is the Word of God, and that there was not one among them whose opinion *on a subject like this* was of any real weight at all, and that, in all honesty, *we were, consequently, logically compelled to accept the testimony of those who say that the Bible is the Inerrant Word of God, and consequently compelled to accept it as the Inerrant Word of God.*

But, while that is so, it is also undoubtedly true, as our text declares, that there are in the Bible many things "hard to be understood." There are in the Bible many statements of historic fact and of doctrine, that it seems difficult to reconcile with the position that this Book has God for its author. There are sometimes in the Bible statements that seem to flatly contradict other statements in the Bible, and it seems at the first glance and sometimes at the second glance and the third glance, that if one statement is true, the other cannot possibly be true; and, therefore, it seems impossible to believe that both statements are from God. And there is, as our text declares, a great temptation for both "the ignorant and the unsteadfast" to "wrest," or more literally translated, "twist," these "things hard to be understood" to "their own destruction," and sometimes to the destruction of others as well as of themselves. I wish to consider those difficulties with you today. What shall we say about them? What shall we do with them? A very easy thing to do with them is to say, what so many superficial students and teachers of the Bible do say, "The *whole* Bible is *not* the Word of God: the Bible *contains* the Word of God. But it also contains much that is not the Word of God and these difficult passages belong to that part which is not the Word of God." Yes, that is an easy thing to say, but it is a lazy thing to say and a superficial thing to say, an unintelligent thing to say, and an irrational and illogical and unscientific thing to say: for we have already proven that not only does "the Bible *contain* the Word of God," but that the Bible *is the Word of God,* and that the *whole* Bible is the Word of God, that every one of the thirty-nine books of the Old Testament and every one of the twenty-seven books of the New Testament is an integral part of the Word of God. So then, what appears at first sight to be an easy way to dispose of these difficulties is found upon more thorough investigation, to be a very hard way, indeed an impossible way for an honest, rational, energetic mind, a mind that thinks things through, and is not satisfied with the lazy way so common in Universities and Theological Seminaries today, the way of *jumping at* conclusions. There is a better way, an intelligent way, a rational way, a manly way, and a Christian way, of dealing with these difficulties.

I. General Statements about These Difficulties

In discovering this "better way" of solving these difficulties, and thus dissolving the mental perplexities that arise from them, let me, first, call your close and careful attention to some general statements that will go a long way towards solving them.

Is the Bible the Inerrant Word of God?

1. First of all, then, let me say that, *From the very nature of the case, difficulties are not to be wondered at, nor to be staggered by, but are to be expected.* Some people are surprised that there are difficulties in the Bible. Some are fairly staggered by the fact that there are difficulties in the Bible. For my part, I would be far more surprised, and far worse staggered, if there were no difficulties in the Bible. What is the Bible? We have seen in the last two addresses that it is the Word of God, that is to say, it is a complete revelation of the mind and will and character and purposes and methods and nature and being of an infinitely great, perfectly wise, and absolutely holy God. And to whom is this revelation made? To you and me. And what are you and I? We are men and women and children; we are all finite beings, persons (all of us) who are very imperfect in intellectual development and, consequently, in knowledge and mental grasp and capacity, and we are also (all of us) imperfect in character and consequently in moral and spiritual discernment. The wisest man on earth, measured on the scale of Eternity and God, is a very young babe; and the holiest man or woman among us, compared with God, is less than an infant in moral and spiritual development, even if we were all God's children, which many of us are not. There must, therefore, from the very necessities of the case, be difficulties in a revelation from such a source made to such persons. *When finite creatures try to understand the infinite Creator, there are bound to be difficulties.* When the very ignorant and limited in knowledge contemplate the utterances of One perfect

Difficulties—General Statements About Them

in knowledge, there must be many "things hard to be understood," and some things which, to their immature and inaccurate minds, appear to be absurd. Why, even some of our exceedingly learned and amazingly wise University Professors confess that they find it extremely hard to understand even Einstein, and he is far from infinite. One man has said that "there are only three men in the world today who understand Einstein, and they don't." You take a bright boy of eight out on a clear day and point to the sun and say, "My boy, that sun is more than ninety-two million miles away," and he is quite likely to think you are kidding. And take him out at night and point to a certain one of the fixed stars and tell him that the light which he now sees from that star, traveling at the incredible velocity at which light travels, left that star six thousand years ago, and he will think you ought to be sent to the insane asylum. But the trouble is not with your statements, but with the immaturity of the boy's mind.

Furthermore, when beings whose moral judgment as to the infinite hatefulness of sin, even in its slightest manifestations, and as to the awfulness of the penalty it deserves and demands, are blunted by their own sinfulness (as the moral judgments of the best of us are), listen to the demands of an infinitely and absolutely holy Being, they are bound to be staggered by some of His demands, and when they consider His actual dealings with sinners, they are bound to be staggered at some of His dealings. These dealings will inevitably appear too stern, too severe, too harsh,

Is the Bible the Inerrant Word of God?

too terrific, too appalling (as, for example, the destruction of the world by the Flood, the blotting out of the Canaanite nations, root and branch, men, women and little children, and the endless torment hereafter of those who persistently reject Christ in the life that now is). But the difficulty is not with the infinitely holy God's dealings with persistent sinners, nor is it with the Bible statement of those dealings, but the whole difficulty is with our moral blindness, which makes it difficult, if not impossible, for us to appreciate the infinite hatefulness of sin, and the infinite glory of Jesus Christ, and the, consequently, infinite damnableness of the sin of rejecting such a Savior as the Lord Jesus is. Probably, the greatest difficulties which the Bible presents are its statements regarding God's judgments upon the Canaanite nations and upon apostate Israel, and especially its statements regarding the future eternal conscious punishment for all who who persistently reject Jesus Christ in the life that now is; and here we see the very simple solution of these most staggering of all Bible difficulties.

It is, therefore, as plain as day that, *There must be difficulties in such a revelation, as we have proven the Bible to be, made to such beings as you and I are.* To me, and to any really thoughtful man, it would be far harder to believe that the Bible is the Word of God if there were nothing in it difficult for me to understand and grasp, than it is to believe the Bible to be the Word of God with all the difficulties anyone has ever been able to conjure up. If you should present to me a book that was as easy for me to understand as the multiplication table, in which I have reveled since I was a little boy, and say to me, "This book is the Word of God; in it God has fully revealed His whole will and wisdom and His own infinite Self," I should be bound to say, "Go away, you're fooling. I cannot believe it. That book is too easy to be a perfect revelation of infinite wisdom and of infinite Being and of an infinite Person." There must be in any complete revelation of the mind and will and character and Being of the Infinite, things very hard for the beginner to understand; yes, for the wisest and best of us to understand. Kent's "Shorter Bible," the Bible with its great and infinite truths expurgated or despiritualized and demoralized and deinfinitized down to the level of a class of mental or moral derelicts, such as fill some of our Universities and Theological Seminaries and Y. W. C. A. Secretarial Schools, is no Bible at all, no full message from God at all, and we should not call it, "The Messages of the Books" of God, but "the miscarriage of modern University thought" that is unable, for lack of moral and spiritual vigor, and sometimes intellectual vigor, to carry Divine thought to a normal birth, and whose thinkings, therefore, on all profoundly moral and spiritual themes, are necessarily all stillborn.

2. The second thing I wish to say about these difficulties in the Bible is that *A difficulty in a doctrine, or a grave objection to a doctrine, does not in any wise prove the doctrine to be untrue.* Many thoughtless people fancy that it does. If they come across some difficulty in the way of believing in the Divine origin

and absolute inerrancy and infallibility of the Bible, they at once conclude that the doctrine is exploded. That is the method of reasoning employed in the Chicago University and Union Seminary in New York, and many other places where our sons and daughters are being educated, or often, to speak more accurately, desiccated, but that is very illogical. Stop a moment and do some clear thinking, and learn to be reasonable and fair. There is scarcely a doctrine in science that is generally believed today that has not had some great difficulty in the way of its acceptance.

When the Copernican theory, now so universally accepted, was first proclaimed, it encountered a very grave difficulty. If this theory were true, the planet Venus should have phases as the moon has, but no phases could be discovered by the most powerful glass then in existence. But the positive argument for the theory was so strong that it was accepted in spite of this apparently unanswerable objection. When a more powerful glass was made, it was found that Venus actually had phases and that the whole difficulty arose, as most all of those in the Bible arise, from man's ignorance of some of the facts in the case.

If we apply to Bible study the common-sense logic recognized in every department of Science (with the exception of Biblical Criticism, if that be a science), then we must demand that if the positive proof of a theory is sufficient and conclusive, it must be believed by rational men, in spite of any number of difficulties in minor details. He is a very shallow thinker indeed who gives up a well-attested truth because there are some apparent facts which he cannot reconcile with that truth. And he is a very shallow Bible scholar who gives up his belief in the Divine origin and inerrancy of the Bible because there are some supposed facts that he cannot reconcile with that doctrine. Alas! there are, in the theological world today, many shallow thinkers of just that sort.

3. The third thing to be said about the Difficulties in the Bible is that, *There are many more, and much greater, difficulties in the way of the doctrine that holds the Bible to be of human origin, and hence fallible, than there are in the way of the doctrine that holds the Bible to be of Divine origin, and hence infallible.* Oftentimes a man will bring you some difficulty and say, "How do you explain that, if the Bible is the Word of God?" and perhaps you may not be able to answer him satisfactorily. Then he thinks he has you cornered, but not at all. Turn on him, and ask him, "How do you account for the fulfilled prophecies of the Bible if it is of *human* origin? How do you account for the marvelous unity of the Bible if it is of *human* origin? How do you account for the inexhaustible depth of the Bible if it is of *human* origin? How do you account for its unique power in lifting man up to God if it is of *human* origin? Above all, How do you account for the clear, ringing, oft repeated testimony of Jesus Christ that every part of the Old Testament, the Law of Moses, the Prophets and Psalms, that 'cannot be broken,' and 'must be fulfilled' to the letter, and that 'heaven and earth (must) pass away' before 'one jot or tittle' passes from the Law re-

vealed in the Pentateuch?" For every insignificant objection that any scholar of the "Modern Critical School," or anyone else, can bring to your view of the Bible, you can bring very many and far more deeply significant objections to his view of the Bible; and any really candid man, who desires to know and obey the truth, will have no difficulty in deciding between the two views.

A young man once came to me to talk about this matter. He had a bright mind and was unusually well read in skeptical and critical and agnostic literature. He told me he had given the matter a great deal of candid and careful thought, and, as a result, he could not believe the Bible was of Divine origin. I asked him, "Why not?" He pointed to a certain teaching of the Bible that he could not and would not believe to be true. I replied, "Suppose, for a moment, that I could not answer that specific difficulty, that would not prove that the Bible is not of Divine origin. I can bring you many things far more difficult to account for on the hypothesis that the Bible is not of Divine origin than this is on the hypothesis that the Bible is of Divine origin. You cannot deny the fact of fulfilled prophecy. How do you account for it if the Bible is not God's Word? You cannot shut your eyes to the marvelous unity of the sixty-six books of the Bible, written by so many different people, under such divergent circumstances, and at periods of time "so remote from one another. How do you account for it, if God is not the real author of the Book back of the forty or more human authors? You cannot deny that the Bible has

Difficulties—General Statements About Them

a power to save men from sin, to bring men peace and joy and hope, to lift men up to God, that all other books taken together do not possess. How do you account for it, if the Bible is not the Word of God, in a sense that no other book is the Word of God?" The objector did not answer. He could not answer. The difficulties that confront one who denies that the Bible is of Divine origin and authority are far more numerous, and vastly more weighty, than those which confront the one who believes it to be of Divine origin and authority.

4. The fourth thing to be said about the difficulties in the Bible is, *The fact that you cannot solve a difficulty does not prove that it cannot be solved, and the fact that you cannot answer an objection does not prove at all that it cannot be answered.* It is remarkable how often we overlook this very evident fact. There are many, who, when they meet a difficulty in the Bible and give it a few moments' thought and can see no possible solution, at once jump at the conclusion that a solution is impossible by anyone, and so they throw up their faith in the Inerrancy of the Bible and its Divine origin. It would seem as if any really normal man would have a sufficient amount of that modesty that is becoming in beings so limited in knowledge as we all undeniably are, to say, "Though *I* see no possible solution to this difficulty, someone a little wiser than I might easily find one."

If we would only bear in mind that we do not know everything as yet, and that there are a great many things that we cannot solve now, that we could very easily solve if we only knew a little more, it would save us from all this wretched and paralyzing folly. Above all, we ought never to forget that there may be a very easy solution in an infinitely wise mind, even to that which to our very best finite wisdom (or ignorance) appears absolutely insoluble. What would we think of a beginner in Algebra, who, having tried in vain for half an hour to solve a difficult problem, declared that there was no possible solution to the problem, *because he could find none?*

A man of unusual experience and ability one day left his work and came a long distance to see me in great perturbation of spirit, because he had discovered what seemed to him a flat contradiction in the Bible. He had remained awake all night thinking about it. It had defied all his attempts at reconciliation, but when he had fully stated the case to me, in a very few moments I showed him a very simple and entirely satisfactory solution of the difficulty. He went away with a happy heart. But why had it not occurred to him at the outset that though it appeared absolutely impossible to him to find a solution that, after all, a solution might be easily discovered by someone else, who knew just a little more than he did? He imagined that the difficulty was an entirely new one, that it had never been discovered by anyone before, but in point of fact it was one that had been faced and answered long before either he or I were born.

5. The fifth thing to be said about the difficulties in the Bible is that, *The seeming defects of the Book are exceedingly insignificant when put in comparison*

with its many and marvelous excellencies. Does it not reveal great perversity, not only of mind but of will and of moral character that men spend so much time expatiating on and magnifying such insignificant points that they consider defects in the Bible, and stubbornly ignore and pass over absolutely unnoticed, the incomparable beauties that adorn and glorify almost every page? Even in some prominent institutions of learning where men are supposed to be taught to appreciate and understand the Bible, and where they are sent to be taught to preach its truths to others, far more time is spent on minute and insignificant points that seem to point toward an entirely or partially human origin of the Bible, than is spent upon studying and understanding and admiring and pondering the unparalleled glories that make this Book stand apart from all other books in the world. What would we think of any man who in studying some great masterpiece of art concentrated his whole attention upon what looked to him like a fly-speck in the corner of the canvas? A large share of the much vaunted "critical study of the Bible" is a laborious and scholarly investigation of supposed fly-specks. The man who is not willing to squander the major portion of his time in this erudite investigation of fly-specks, but prefers to devote it to the study of the unrivaled beauties and majestic splendors and infinite glories of the Book, is counted, in some quarters, as not being "scholarly" and "up to date."

6. The sixth thing to be said about the difficulties in the Bible is, *They have far more weight with*

Is the Bible the Inerrant Word of God?

superficial readers of the Bible than with profound students of the Bible. Take a man like the late Colonel Ingersoll, who was densely ignorant of the real contents and meaning of the Bible, or that class of modern preachers who read the Bible for the most part for the sole purpose of finding texts to serve as pegs upon which to hang their own profound ideas and musings, to such superficial readers of the Bible, these difficulties seem of immense importance, indeed to them they are the only things in the Bible that are of any real importance. But with the "blessed man," the man who has learned to "meditate" upon the Word of God "day and night" (Ps. 1:1-3) they have scarcely any weight at all. That rare man of God, George Müller, who had carefully studied the whole Bible and every verse in it from the first verse of Genesis to the last verse of the Revelation of Jesus Christ" more than one hundred times, was not at all disturbed by any difficulties he encountered. But to the man who is reading it through for the first or second time there are many things that perplex and, it may be, stagger him.

7. The seventh and last thing to be said about the Difficulties in the Bible is, *They rapidly disappear upon careful and prayerful study.* How many things there are in the Bible that once puzzled and staggered you and me, but which have long since been perfectly cleared up and no longer present any difficulty whatever? Every year of our study has found these difficulties disappearing more and more rapidly. At first

Difficulties—General Statements About Them

they went by ones, and then by twos, and then by dozens, and then by scores. Is it not reasonable to suppose that the difficulties that even yet remain will all disappear on still further study?

CHAPTER IV

DIFFICULTIES IN THE BIBLE: WHAT SHALL WE DO WITH THEM?

"Many therefore of his disciples, when they heard this, said, This is a hard saying; who can hear it? . . . From that time many of his disciples went back, and walked no more with him."—John 6:60, 66.

Our subject this morning is: "Difficulties in the Bible: What shall we do with them?" You will find the text in John 6:60, 66: "Many therefore of His disciples, when they heard this, said, This is a hard saying; who can hear it? . . . From that time many of His disciples went back, and walked no more with Him."

There are many today who stumble at things they find in the Bible. They say that these things cannot be God's Word, and so they give up the Bible and, ultimately, they give up Jesus Christ; for anyone who gives up the Bible is bound to give up Jesus Christ sooner or later. They may use His name still, and speak in a very complimentary way about Him, and they may call themselves "Christians" and even pose as preachers, but they have really given up Him; they have given up the only Real Christ there is—the Christ of the Bible. Any other Christ than the Christ of the Bible is a fictitious Christ, a pure figment of the imagination, a false Christ, an Anti-Christ. They give up, first, His Virgin Birth, then they give up His literal Resurrection from the Dead, then they give up His Atoning Death, then they have no Christ left, only a shadow, an empty dream. The Real Christ has gone. They have no Real Christ, Christ Jesus, and they are "without Christ . . . having no hope, and without God in the world." (Eph. 2:12.) They are doomed and ultimately damned.

Now, this is no new thing. It is not at all peculiar to our day, as many seem to fancy. It is not peculiar to the twentieth century, nor to the nineteenth century. In our text we see the same thing in the first century. We see that when the Lord Jesus Himself was here on earth, those who had been "His disciples," those who had followed Him, those who had come to Him and *professed to be "learners" in His school,* stumbled, even at what He Himself said, and shook their heads and said, "This is a hard saying; who can hear it?" and then we read, "From that time many of His disciples went back, and walked no more with Him." If men who professed to be disciples of Christ and saw Him with their own eyes and "beheld His miracles," and who on the immediately preceding day had been of the five thousand who saw the five small loaves and two small fishes multiplying in His hands, stumbled at something He said, just because, with their dull, puny brains they could not take it in and, therefore, stupidly and wickedly threw it overboard, because, as Jesus Himself said to them, they had not faith (vs. 64) and, therefore, had not sense enough to just trust the

Son of God, when they could not see, is it any wonder if men today are so foolish as to throw the words of Jesus Christ overboard because they cannot fully take them in, and throw the Bible overboard because there are in it what appear to them, "hard sayings"?

There are, as we saw last Sunday, Difficulties in the Bible, real Difficulties. What shall we do with them? How shall we deal with them? Last Sunday I gave you seven general statements about these Difficulties that will go a long way toward solving them for you, and many of you told me afterward that you were greatly helped. One young woman came up and said, "That sermon was just for me." She was in school and was being bothered by things she heard there, as so many young men and young women today are being bothered by what shallow and ignorant and self-sufficient teachers and professors in High Schools, Colleges and Universities are saying.

I. *How to Deal with the Difficulties in the Bible*

But what shall we do with these Difficulties? How shall we deal with them when we meet them?

1. First of all, let me say, *Let us deal with any Difficulty and every Difficulty we meet in the Bible with perfect honesty.* Whenever you find a Difficulty in the Bible, frankly acknowledge it, do not try to obscure it, do not try to dodge it, do not evade it. Evasion never pays. Be honest through and through; perfect honesty and frankness always win out in the long run. Look the Difficulty frankly and fearlessly square in the face, admit it frankly to whoever men-

tions it. If you cannot give a good, square, honest explanation, do not attempt any explanation at all. Untold harm has been done by those who, in their zeal for the infallibility of the Bible, have attempted explanations of Difficulties which do not commend themselves to the honest, fair-minded man. People have naturally thought that if these are the best explanations that can be given, then there are really no explanations at all, and the Bible, instead of being helped, has been injured by the unintelligent zeal of foolish friends. Foolish friends of the Bible have done far more to discredit it with men and women who think for themselves than the bitterest enemies have ever done. If you are really convinced that the Bible is the Word of God, you can far better afford to wait for an honest solution of a Difficulty than you can afford to attempt a solution that is evasive and unsatisfactory. Let us hate all manner of evasion and lying. A "pious lie" is the most impious and the most destructive of all lies.

2. In the second place, *Let us deal with any Difficulty we meet in the Bible with that humility that becomes all persons of such limited understanding as we all are.* Recognize the limitations of your own mind and knowledge, and do not for a moment imagine that there is no solution just because you have found none. There is, in all probability, a very simple solution, even when you can find no solution at all.

3. In the third place, *Let us deal with every Difficulty we meet in the Bible with indomitable determination.* Make up your mind that you will find the solu-

tion, if you possibly can, no matter what amount of time and study and hard thinking it may require. The Difficulties in the Bible are our Heavenly Father's challenge to us to set our brains to work, and to keep them at work until we have solved the puzzle. Do not give up searching for a solution because you cannot find one in five minutes or ten minutes or ten days. Ponder over it and work over it for days, if necessary. The work will do you more good than the solution does. There is a solution somewhere and you will find it, if you will only search for it long enough and hard enough. I thank God for the hardest puzzles I have found in the Bible, that have made me think and think and think, and dig and dig and dig, and ransack the Bible. That is why I am here today, in my present position of rare and joyous opportunity.

4. In the fourth place, *Deal with every Difficulty you find in the Bible with perfect fearlessness.* Oh! there are so many students of the Bible who have horrid skeletons and frightful ghosts in the closets of their Bible thinking. There are passages here and there at which they are afraid to look. They are afraid someone in their Sunday-School class will spring some question upon them about them. I do not like ghosts. I love to run them down. I hurt a ghost badly one night, when I was a boy, by kicking him in the stomach; and the ghost proved to be only a neighbor boy with a pumpkin lantern on his pumpkin head, and a sheet over both the lantern and himself. That is about all that there is, usually, to these ghosts in our Bible study,

Difficulties—What Shall We Do With Them?

the seeming Difficulties that nearly frighten the wits out of many of us.

Some years ago there was a ghost that haunted a graveyard in Georgia. Many had seen this ghost in the weird hours of the night running along the top of the graveyard wall. One night, a doctor driving by saw the ghost. He could scarcely believe his eyes. There it was, all white and active. He was a brave man. He fastened his horse and ran after the ghost. The ghost ran along the wall and jumped down on the other side, and the doctor sprang over after him. The ghost dodged in and out among the tombs, with the doctor in hot pursuit. There was a flat grave-stone underneath which the water had washed away some of the earth. The ghost plunged into this hole. It certainly was a ghost, going back into its grave. But the doctor was brave. He was no quitter. He plunged his hand into the grave, and caught the ghost by the heel and pulled it out. The ghost was an insane woman in a nightgown. She had been running loose through the Cemetery frightening the wits out of silly folk. Do not be afraid of ghosts anywhere; and especially do not be afraid of ghosts in your Bible study. Do not be frightened when you find a Difficulty, no matter how unanswerable or how inexplicable or how insurmountable it may appear at first sight. Thousands of men have found just such Difficulties before you were born. Not only that, but they have seen this same Difficulty that now frightens you. These Difficulties were all seen hundreds of years ago, and still the Old Book stands. The Bible that has already stood eighteen centuries of rigid examination, and also of incessant and awful assault, is not likely to go down before your discoveries, or even before the discharge of any "modern," "scholarly," "critical" guns (in which they certainly use neither smokeless nor noiseless powder) nor before the poison gases of "Modern Criticism" either, which is usually found to be only "hot air" after all. To one who is at all familiar with the history of "critical" attacks on the Bible, the childlike confidence of these self-sufficient "modern" (destructive) "critics," who think they are going to annihilate the Bible at last, is both amazing and amusing.

While we were going round the world, almost everywhere that we held meetings, in Australia, New Zealand, Tasmania, India, England, Scotland, Ireland, Wales, and all over America, I had a question box once a week, or oftener, in which people could place any difficulty they found in the Bible, and I promised to answer it, *if I could.* After awhile I found that the same questions and problems came up everywhere. People would put in questions that they imagined were new, but they were all gray-headed. Until, at last, I was quite persuaded that Solomon was right when he said, "There is no new thing under the sun" (Eccles. 1:9), at least in Bible Difficulties. And some of our vastly learned Theological Professors of the *"Modern Critical School"* are trotting out these old, dilapidated, wind-broken hacks of horses, poor ringboned, spavined, old plugs, on the theological race course with a joyous assurance that they have found at last a pure-blooded young Arabian of matchless speed.

Difficulties—What Shall We Do With Them?

When we were holding meetings in Massey Hall, Toronto, a young theological student, who was deeply concerned about my need of intellectual illumination, wrote me a pathetic note urging me to attend the lectures of a much admired young Professor who was then teaching in Knox College, that I might learn what real "modern thinking" and "scholarship" had to say about the Bible. Bless his dear young heart, I had heard before, in Germany, the source of all this sort of stuff (and elsewhere) all the Professor was retailing in Toronto, as a feeble echo of what was being echoed in Scotland from Germany, whence the original voice came, I say I had heard it all before, while the brilliant Professor was still in pantalets in bonnie Scotland. I met the Professor himself at dinner a few nights later, and told him of his fresh and callow student, and we had a good laugh over it.

There is nothing to be afraid of in any of these Difficulties. It has been proved, beyond the possibility of reasonable doubt, that the whole Bible is the Inerrant Word of God, so we may look every apparently portentous Difficulty square in the face, with absolute and well founded confidence that some day, if not today, a complete solution will be found.

5. In the fifth place, *Let us deal with the Difficulties we find in the Bible with undiscouraged and untiring patience.* Do not be discouraged in the least, if some Difficulty that you discover, or that someone else fires at you, does not disappear at the first hour's consideration of it, or in a day. Have you never had problems in other lines of study that you could not solve even

in a year? If not, you have never done any deep studying along any line. If some Difficulty persistently defies your very hardest efforts to solve it, lay it aside for awhile and ponder other things. Very likely, when you come back to it, it will have disappeared, and you will wonder how you were ever perplexed by it.

A friend wrote me a few years ago about an entirely different sort of Difficulty that had arisen in my own work and, apparently, a very serious Difficulty. "If I were you," he wrote, "I would not do anything about it. Time is a great healer." I took his advice and dismissed the matter for a time, in fact I never did anything about it, and time did prove to be a great healer. The Difficulty entirely evaporated beneath the genial rays of the march of time. So it will be with many of your most disconcerting Bible Difficulties. Be patient and they will vanish of themselves; and the bugbear you once trembled at, you will now laugh at.

6. In the sixth place, and this is of tremendous importance, *Deal with all Bible Difficulties Scripturally.* If you find an apparently staggering Difficulty in one part of the Bible, look for some other passage of Scripture to throw light upon it and solve it. The best solvent of Bible Difficulties is found in the Bible itself. Nothing explains Scripture like Scripture. That is one of the countless practical proofs of the Divine origin of the Bible, that "all Scripture is God breathed." Time and time again, people have come to me with some Difficulty in the Bible that had greatly staggered them, and almost floored them, and implored me for a solution, and I simply pointed them to some other

Difficulties—What Shall We Do With Them?

passage in the Book whose clearer light has scattered all the mists and apparent miasma that seemed to gather thick about the passage that troubled. The darkness vanished, and the glorious day dawned. The entrance of God's words had given light; it had given understanding unto the simple (Ps. 119:130).

7. In the seventh and last place, *Deal with every Difficulty prayerfully.* It is simply wonderful how Difficulties dissolve when one looks at them on his knees. It is an easy way to "dissolve doubts" and explain "dark sentences." Daniel found it so many centuries and chiliads ago (Dan. 5:12, cf. Dan. 6:10). There is a glorious alchemy about prayer that transforms the darkest and most bewildering Difficulties into clear shining and illuminating truth, that transforms "stones of stumbling" into the many jeweled walls of the New Jerusalem, with its endless day and "no night there." It is well, as you read your Bible, not only to pray, "Open thou my eyes, that I may behold wondrous things out of thy law" but, also, "Open thou my eyes that I may see through and through the rough oyster shell of seeming difficulty to the glorious pearl of lustrous truth within." Not only does God, in answer to prayer, open our eyes "to behold wondrous things" out of His law, but he also opens our eyes to look through a Difficulty that before we prayed seemed impenetrable. One great reason why so many "Modern Bible Scholars" have learned to be destructive critics is because they have forgotten how to pray.

II. Classes of Difficulties

I have a little time left to speak of the various Classes of Difficulties. All the Difficulties found in the Bible can be included under ten general heads.

1. *The first Class of Difficulties are those that arise from the text from which our English Bible was translated.* No one, as far as I know, holds that the Authorized Version, or any English translation of the Bible, is absolutely infallible and inerrant. The doctrine held by me and by many others who have given years to careful and thorough study of the Bible is, that the Scriptures *as originally given* were absolutely infallible and Inerrant, and that our English translation is a *substantially* accurate rendering of the Scriptures as originally given. We do not possess the original manuscripts of the Bible. These original manuscripts were copied many, many times with great care and exactness, but, naturally, some errors crept into the copies that were made. We now possess so many good copies that by comparing one with another, we can tell with great precision just what the original text was. Indeed, for all practical purposes the original text is now settled. There is not one important doctrine that hangs upon any doubtful or uncertain reading of the text. But when our Authorized Version was made, some of the best manuscripts that we now have were not within the reach of the translators, and the science of textual criticism was not so perfected then as it is today, and so the translation was made from an im-

Difficulties—What Shall We Do With Them?

perfect text. Not a few of the apparent Difficulties in the Bible arise from this source.

For example, we are told in Jno. 5:4 that "an angel went down at a certain season into the pool, and troubled the water: whosoever then first ·after the troubling of the water stepped in was made whole of whatsoever disease he had." This statement, for many reasons, seems improbable and difficult to believe, but, upon investigation, we find that it is all a mistake of the copyist. Some early copyist, reading John's account, added in the margin his explanation of the healing properties of this intermittent medicinal spring. A later copyist embodied this marginal note in the body of the text, and so it came to be handed down and got into the Authorized Version. Very properly, it has been omitted from the Revised Version.

The discrepancies in figures in different accounts of the same events, as, for example, the differences in the ages of some of the kings as given in the texts of Kings and Chronicles, may arise from the same cause, errors of copyists. Such an error in the matter of figures could very easily be made, as in the Hebrew numbers are denoted by letters, and letters that appear very much alike have a very different value as figures. For example, the first letter in the Hebrew alphabet denotes "one," and with two little points above it, not larger than flyspecks, it denotes a "thousand." The twenty-third or last letter of the Hebrew alphabet denotes "four hundred," but the eighth letter of the Hebrew alphabet, that looks very much like it and could easily be mistaken for it, denotes "eight." A very slight error of the copyist would therefore make an utter change in the figures. The remarkable thing, when one contemplates the facts in the case, is that so few errors of this kind have been made, and we are constantly getting proof that the figures we fancied were wrong are really correct.

2. *The second Class of Difficulties are those that arise from inaccurate translations.* For example, in Matt. 12:40 Jonah is spoken of as being "in the *whale's* belly." Many a skeptic has made merry over the thought of a whale with the peculiar construction of its mouth and throat swallowing a man, but if the skeptic had only taken the trouble to look the matter up, he would have found that the word translated "whale" really means "sea monster," without any definition as to the character of the sea monster. So, the whole difficulty arose from the translator's mistakes and the skeptic's ignorance. There are many skeptics today who are so densely ignorant of matters clearly understood by many Sunday-School children that they are still harping, in the name of "scholarship," on this supposed error in the Bible. One of the best known professors in Union Theological Seminary, in New York, one of the most popular of "modernist" preachers trotted this out in an address last Oct. 23, 1921. In regard to this particular Difficulty, it may be still further said that there are whales of another species than those known some years ago (when the critics first urged this objection to the historical credibility of the Bible) that could swallow a man whole, and have swallowed a man

Difficulties—What Shall We Do With Them?

whole, and a man has been rescued alive from "the belly of a whale."

3. *The third Class of Difficulties are those that arise from false interpretations of the Bible.* What the Bible teaches is one thing, and what men interpret it to mean is oftentimes something widely different. Many Difficulties that we have with the Bible arise not from what the Bible actually says, but from what men interpret it to mean. A striking illustration of this is found in the first chapter of Genesis. If we were to take the interpretation put upon this chapter by many interpreters, it might be somewhat difficult to reconcile it with much that modern science regards as established. But the difficulty is not with what the first chapter of Genesis says, but with the interpretation that is put upon it. There is no contradiction whatever between *what is really proven* by science and *what is really said* in the first chapter of Genesis.

4. *The fourth Class of Difficulties are those that arise from a wrong conception of the Bible.* Many think that when you say the Bible is the Word of God, that it is of Divine origin and authority, that you mean that God is the speaker in every utterance that it contains, but this is not at all what is meant. Oftentimes, the Bible simply records what others say—what good men say, what bad men say, what inspired men say, what uninspired men say, what angels and demons say, and even what The Devil himself says. The record of what they said is from God, God's Word, and is absolutely true, but what those other persons are recorded

as saying may be true or may not be true. It is true that they said it, but what they said may not be true.

For example, The devil is recorded, in Gen. 3:4, as saying: "Ye shall not surely die." It is true that The Devil said it, but what The Devil said is not true, but an infamous lie that shipwrecked our race. That The Devil said it is God's Word, but what The Devil said is not God's word, but The Devil's word. It is not God's truth, but The Devil's lie. It is God's word that this lie was The Devil's word.

Very many careless readers of the Bible do not notice who is talking—God, good men, bad men, inspired men, uninspired men, angels or Devil. They will tear a verse right out of its context, regardless of the speaker, and say: "There, God said that," but God said nothing of the kind. God says *The Devil* said it, or a bad man said it, or a good man said it, or an inspired man said it, or an uninspired man said it, or an angel said it. What God says is true, viz., that The Devil said it, or that someone else said it, but what they said may not be true.

It is very common to hear men quote what Eliphaz, Bildad, or Zophar said to Job as if it were necessarily God's own word because it is recorded in the Bible, in spite of the fact that God definitely disavowed their teaching and said to them: "Ye have not spoken of Me the thing which is right" (Jno. 42:7). It is true that these men said the thing that God records them as saying, but, oftentimes, they gave the truth a twist, and said what is not right. A very large share of our Difficulties thus arise from not noticing who is speak-

Difficulties—What Shall We Do With Them?

ing. The Bible always makes it plain who is speaking, and we should always note carefully who is speaking.

5. *The fifth Class of Difficulties are those that arise from the language in which the Bible was written.* The Bible is a book for all ages and for all kinds of people, and, therefore, it was written in the language that continues the same and is understood by all, the language of the common people and of appearances (phenomena). It was not written in the terminology of science. It is one of the perfections of the Bible that it was not written in the terminology of modern science. If the Bible had been written in the terminology of modern science, it would never have been understood until the present day, and, even now, it would be understood only by a few. Furthermore, as science and its terminology are constantly changing, the Bible, if written in the terminology of the science of today, would be out of date in a few years from now, but being written in just the language chosen, it has proved the Book for all ages, all lands and all conditions of men.

Other Difficulties, from the language in which the Bible was written, arise from the fact that large portions of the Bible are poetical, and are written in the language of poetry, the language of feeling, passion, imagination and figure. Now, if a man is hopelessly prosaic, he will inevitably find Difficulties with these poetical portions of the inspired Word.

6. *The sixth Class of Difficulties are those that arise from our defective knowledge of the history, geography and usages of Bible times.* We have an

illustration of this in Acts 13:7. Here, Luke speaks of "the deputy," or, more accurately, "the proconsul" (see Revised Version) of Cyprus. Roman provinces were of two classes, imperial and senatorial. The ruler of an imperial province was called a "proprætor," of a senatorial province a "proconsul." Up to a comparatively recent date, according to the best information we had, Cyprus was an imperial province and, therefore, its ruler would be a "proprætor," but Luke calls him a "proconsul." This certainly seemed like a clear case of error on Luke's part, and even conservative commentators in former days felt forced to admit that Luke was in slight error, and the destructive critics were delighted to find this "mistake." But further and more thorough investigation has brought to light the fact that just at the time of which Luke wrote, the Senate had made an exchange with the Emperor, whereby Cyprus had become a senatorial province, and, therefore, its ruler a "proconsul"; and Luke was exactly and minutely correct, after all, and the very "scholarly" literary critics were themselves in error in their criticism. The mistake was theirs and not Luke's.

Time and time again, further researches and discoveries, geographical, historical and archaeological, have vindicated the Bible and confounded the critics. All the discoveries of modern archaeological research have justified the Bible statements and exposed the folly of "The Higher Critics." That has happened time and time again, until nothing is left of the com-

Difficulties—What Shall We Do With Them?

posite theory of the Pentateuch, and the theory of its late origin as originally taught and defined.

The book of Daniel has, naturally, been one of the books that infidels and destructive critics have most hated. One of their strongest arguments against its authenticity and veracity was that such a person as Belshazzar was unknown to history, and that all historians agreed that Nabonidus was the last king of Babylon, and that he was absent from the City when it was captured, and so Belshazzar must be a purely mythical character and the whole story legendary and not historical. Their argument seemed very strong; in fact, it seemed unanswerable. But Sir H. Rawlinson discovered at Mugheir, and other Chaldean sites, clay cylinders on which Belshazzar (Belsaruzur) is named by Nabonidus himself as his eldest son. Doubtless, he reigned as regent in the City during his father's absence, an indication of which we have in the Bible account in his proposal to make Daniel *"third ruler* in the kingdom" (Dan. 5:16)—he himself being *second ruler* in the kingdom, Daniel then would be next to himself. So the Bible was vindicated, and the critics put to shame.

It is not so long since the destructive critics asserted most positively that Moses could not have written the Pentateuch, because writing was unknown in his day, but recent discoveries have proved, beyond a question, that writing far antedates the time of Moses. So, the destructive critics have been compelled to give up their argument, though they have had the bad grace to hold on stubbornly to their conclusion, even though the foundation upon which the conclusion was built was gone.

7. *The seventh Class of Difficulties are those that arise from the ignorance of conditions under which books were written and commands given.* For example, to one ignorant of the conditions, God's commands to Israel as to the extermination of the Canaanites seem cruel and horrible, but when one understands the moral condition to which those nations had sunken, and the utter hopelessness of reclaiming them and the weakness of the Israelites themselves, the total extermination of the Canaanites seems to have been an act of mercy to all succeeding generations, and even to themselves.

8. *The eighth Class of Difficulties are those that arise from the many-sidedness of the Bible.* The broadest minded man is one-sided, but the truth is many-sided, and the Bible is all-sided. So, to our narrow thoughts one part of the Bible often seems to contradict another part. For example, men as a rule are either Calvinistic or Arminian in their mental make-up, and some portions of the Bible are decidedly Calvinistic and present great Difficulties to the Arminian type of mind, while other portions are decidedly Arminian and present great Difficulties to the Calvinistic type of mind, but both sides are true. Many men in our day are broad-minded enough to grasp at the same time the Calvinistic side of the truth and the Arminian side of the truth, but some are not, and so the Bible perplexes, puzzles and bewilders them, but

the trouble is not with the Bible, but with their own lack of capacity for comprehensive thought.

9. *The ninth Class of Difficulties are those that arise from the fact that the Bible has to do with the infinite, and our minds are finite.* It is necessarily difficult to put the facts of infinite being in such a way that they can be grasped by the limited capacity of our finite intelligence, just as it would be difficult to put the ocean into a pint cup. To this Class of Difficulties belong those connected with the Bible doctrine of the Trinity and with the Bible doctrine of the twofold nature of Jesus Christ, who was at the same time "very God of very God" and real man. To those who forget that God is infinite, the doctrine of the Trinity seems like the mathematical monstrosity of making one equal three. But when one bears in mind that the doctrine of the Trinity is an attempt to put into forms of finite thought the facts of infinite being, and into material forms of expression the facts of the spirit, the Difficulties vanish. The simplicity of the Unitarian conception of God arises from its shallowness.

10. *The tenth Class of Difficulties are those that arise from the dullness of our spiritual perceptions.* The man who is farthest advanced spiritually is still so immature that he cannot expect to see everything yet as an absolutely holy God sees it, unless he takes it upon simple faith in Him. To this Class of Difficulties belong those connected with the Bible doctrine of eternal punishment. It oftentimes seems to us as if this doctrine cannot be true, must not be true, but the whole Difficulty arises from the fact that we are still

so blind spiritually that we have no adequate conception of the awfulness of sin, and, especially, of the awfulness of the sin of rejecting the infinitely glorious Son of God. But when we become so holy, so like God, that we see the enormity of sin as He sees it, we shall have no difficulty whatever with the doctrine of eternal punishment.

As we look back over the ten Classes of Difficulties, we see that they *all* arise from our own imperfection, and not one of them from the imperfection of the Bible. The Bible is perfect, but we are imperfect and, therefore, have difficulty with it. As we grow more and more into the perfection of God, into His intellectual perfection and, especially, into His moral perfection, our Difficulties grow ever less and less, and so we are forced to conclude that when we become as perfect as God is, we shall have no Difficulties whatever with the Bible.

CHAPTER V

WHAT TO DO WITH THE BIBLE

"But know this, that in the last days grievous times shall come. . . . Yea, and all that would live godly in Christ Jesus shall suffer persecution. But evil men and impostors shall wax worse and worse, deceiving and being deceived. But abide thou in the things which thou hast learned and hast been assured of, knowing of whom thou hast learned them; and that from a babe thou hast known the sacred writings which are able to make thee wise unto salvation through faith which is in Christ Jesus. Every scripture is inspired of God and is profitable for teaching, for reproof, for correction, for instruction which is in righteousness: that the man of God may be complete, furnished completely unto every good work."—2 Tim. 3:1, 12–17.

Our subject this morning is, "What to do with the Bible." You will find the text which contains the substance of what I have to say, in 2 Tim. 3:1, 12–17:— "But know this, that in the last days grievous times shall come . . . Yea, and all that would live godly in Christ Jesus shall suffer persecution. But evil men and impostors shall wax worse and worse, deceiving and being deceived. But abide thou in the things which thou hast learned and hast been assured of, knowing of whom thou hast learned them; and that from a babe thou hast known the sacred writings which are able to make thee wise unto salvation through faith which is in Christ Jesus. Every Scripture is inspired of God and is profitable for teaching, for reproof, for correction, for instruction which is in righteousness: that the man of God may be complete, furnished completely unto every good work."—2 Tim. 3:1, 12-17.

Paul here tells Timothy of the "difficult times" that are coming, times of great peril and testing. He tells him of the certainty of persecution for those who are faithful to Christ Jesus. Then he tells of the great increase of evil men and subtle errorists, both deceiving themselves and also deceiving others. It is an exceedingly dark picture that he draws, but it is a very accurate and graphic picture of our own times. It is a startlingly accurate picture of our own times. It is a picture to fill one with apprehension and dismay, were Paul to stop here, but Paul did not stop here. No, he went on to say, in substance, "But, Timothy, even with these exceedingly dark days ahead, there is nothing to be afraid of, there is a path of perfect safety, though perils lie on every side. That path of safety is found in the study of, and trust in, and obedience to, the Holy Scriptures, which are *"inspired of God"* (that is, to translate more literally, *"God-breathed"*). However, many and however subtle false teachers may be, the Holy Scriptures are able to make thee wise unto salvation through the faith which is in Christ Jesus. Furthermore, Timothy, you can put perfect confidence in *these Scriptures,* for they are *God-breathed,* and are profitable for every needed use, for teaching, for reproof, for correction and instruction in righteousness, and through the study of these, no matter how the night darkens and the perils increase, the man of God

What to Do with the Bible

will be complete, furnished completely unto every good work."

We are living today in the days that Paul so accurately pictured nearly nineteen centuries ago—the evil men, *the spiritual jugglers* (which is the exact force of the word translated "impostors"), and spiritual impostors of all sorts, are increasing at an appalling rate, and they are becoming more and more cunningly, and more and more shamelessly, "worse and worse." You will find them wherever you go, in the country as well as the city, and in the foreign field as well as at home, in China and Japan and India as well as in America. How shall anyone who sincerely desires to serve God, and accomplish the very best results for Him, find safety? What shall he do? Our text answers the question. You will find safety in the Book, the one Book of God, "the Sacred Writings," the Writings *"inspired of God,"* the Bible; the Bible which we have conclusively proven to be the Inerrant Word of God. Paul, of course, had the Old Testament books in view when he wrote these words. It was these Timothy had "known from a babe." But if what Paul says in these words is true of the thirty-nine books of the Old Testament, and it is, it is certainly true of the twenty-seven books of the New Testament. The Bible, *if a man use it aright,* will make a man perfectly safe, no matter how error may abound and how subtle it may be. And the Bible, if properly used, will make him to be thoroughly equipped for God's service. But how must we use this Book to be safe in these times of increasing darkness and peril, and to be completely equipped in a time when so many workers, yes, even so many ministers and theological professors, are making an utter shipwreck of their usefulness? This exceedingly important question is answered in the Book itself, indeed is very largely answered in my text. So my subject this morning is, "What to do with the Bible." In our recent addresses we have clearly proven the Bible to be *the Inerrant Word of God* and on the basis of that demonstrated fact, we take up the subject of "What to do with the Bible," what shall we do with the Book which is proven to be the Inerrant Word of God?

I. Believe the Bible

The first thing to do with the Bible, if we are to find safety in it from the multiplying errors and moral perils, and other perils of the day, and if we are to have complete furnishment through the Bible for every good work, is **to** *Believe the Bible,* Believe the whole Bible, for, as we have seen, the whole Bible is the Word of God. When you allow yourself to entertain doubts as to the absolute reliability of any statement of the Bible, the Bible loses its power to save you from that error which that statement exposes. The Unitarian understands that, and so he seeks to undermine our faith in the Gospel of John. The Universalist understands it, too, and so he seeks to undermine our faith in those passages which clearly set forth the doom of the impenitent. The Christian Scientist understands it, and so he seeks to undermine our faith in those parts of the Bible which lay bare the disgusting folly and

What to Do with the Bible

the many glaring falsehoods of Christian Science. The Spiritualist and the Theosophist understand it, and so they seek to undermine our faith in those passages that lay bare the Satanic origin of those thoroughly demoniacal creeds. Professor Kent and his colleagues, who hate the precious doctrine of the substitutionary character of the death of Christ and the atoning value of His shed blood, and allied doctrines, understand it also, and so they bring out their "Shorter Bible," that calmly eliminates the passages that contain these doctrines. As, for example, by omitting entirely from the 3rd chapter of Romans the 25th and 26th verses, the very heart of that wondrous chapter. And this so-called "Shorter Bible" eliminates these passages, and kindred passages, without one particle of manuscript evidence, without one particle of textual, or other sanely critical reason for such elimination. Believe the Bible, that is the first thing to do with it, believe the whole Bible. Believe, not a man-made "Shorter Bible," but a God-made full Bible. Listen to the text again, *"Every* Scripture is inspired of God (God-breathed), and is profitable for teaching, for reproof, for correction, for instruction in righteousness." The Revisers tried to tinker up that verse and make it read differently, by changing the position of the word "is" in the verse, but this they did without a particle of reason, indeed against all reason, *there not being one single instance of such a construction of a sentence to be found anywhere else in the Bible.* But even were we to admit the correctness of the change, even then they have failed to accomplish their object, for there can be no doubt that by "every Scripture inspired of God," if Paul had used that phrase, he would have meant every Scripture of the Old Testament. *Believe the whole Bible.* The proof that the whole Bible is the Word of God is, as we have recently seen, unanswerable and, therefore, the whole Bible is worthy of your absolute confidence. When you begin to doubt any part of it, look out. Doubt of that kind is a "leaven" that grows with surprising rapidity, until it has "leavened the whole lamp." When the destructive critics began their work, they began with portions of the Bible that did not seem so vital, but they went on and on, until now they do not hesitate to discredit everything that is most fundamental. Yes, they even discredit the teachings of Jesus Christ Himself, and not only discredit His teachings but discredit the conduct of our glorious Lord and Savior, Jesus Christ. They do not hesitate to demand that we accept their authority and Inerrancy instead of the authority and Inerrancy of Jesus Christ.

Twenty-five or thirty years ago, I was talking with a good man and a sound man, but not a very clear and far-seeing thinker, about the destructive criticism as it stood then. He said to me, in speaking of some of the more mildly destructive theories, "They tell me it does not touch any vital point anyway, and what difference does it make whether Isaiah wrote the later chapters of the book or whether someone else wrote them?" I told him that this was only the entering wedge, and I urged him to look to where it would lead and where it would end. It has led to and ended

What to Do with the Bible

exactly where I then predicted it would. Any smallest insect of destructive criticism is like the little borer ant which gets into the underpinning of Hawaiian houses and bores and bores away unseen, until suddenly the whole house collapses. Believe the Bible, *believe the whole Bible*. It will prove in the ultimate outcome every time that it is either the whole Bible or else no Bible at all. Today it is Professor Kent as he was fifteen years or so ago, tomorrow it is Professor Kent as he is today, next day it is a critic who puts Bob Ingersoll all in the shade, and the next day it will be the Devil himself, laughing and jibbering and jabbering and mocking, saying, "Yea, hath God said?" (Gen. 3:1.)

But exactly what is involved in believing the whole Bible?

1. In the first place, *Believe its every statement, its historical statements, its doctrinal statements, its statements of every kind.* Every statement that the Bible makes (that is, the Bible as originally given) is absolutely true. Of course, as we have seen in a recent sermon, that does not mean that every statement that every one is recorded in the Bible as making is necessarily true, for, as we saw then, the Bible records some statements that the Devil made and uninspired men made, but the Bible statement that the Devil or these uninspired men made these statements is absolutely true.

2. In the second place, *Believe absolutely its every Promise.* Risk anything and everything on its every promise. Take every promise as meaning all that it

says. Never discount the least bit any promise in the Word of God. Some of these promises are stupendous, some of them seem incredible, but, nevertheless, believe them in all their height and length and depth and breadth, for they are God's Word.

Of course, we should note carefully to whom the promise is made, for some of the promises of God's Word were made to individuals and some of them were made to the Jews as Jews, and we should believe them only as applying to those to whom they were made. The Bible is always careful to make clear to whom any promise is made, and every promise made to believers in Jesus Christ belongs to every believer in Christ, if he will only trust it and appropriate it. The promises made to Jewish *believers* belong to Gentile believers as well, for God distinctly tells us in His own Word that *"in Christ Jesus"* "there can be neither Jew nor Gentile" (Gal. 3:28), and it says, still further, "and if ye are Christ's, *then are ye Abraham's seed, heirs according to promise*" (Gal. 3:29).

3. In the third place, *Believe absolutely every Warning in the Bible.* We should believe the warnings of the Bible as well as its promises. We should believe what it says about the punishment of sin just as firmly as what it says about the reward of righteousness. We should believe what it says about the guilt and awful doom of the unbeliever as unquestioningly as what it says about the wondrous privileges and eternal rewards and glory of the believer. We should believe what it says about judgment as confidently as what it says about salvation. We should believe what it says about

hell as firmly as we believe what it says about heaven. Here we see the inconsistency of many people and many preachers today. They accept all the Bible has to say about heaven and glowingly expatiate upon what it says about heaven, but when they come to the Bible's equally clear and definite statements about hell, they qualify them and tone them down, or throw them overboard altogether. We have exactly the same reason for believing in an eternal hell of conscious and awful suffering as we have for believing in an eternal heaven of unutterable joy and glory; namely, God says so. There is no other proof that there is a heaven awaiting the believer than the same proof that there is a hell of appalling conscious agony, that will never end, awaiting every one who persistently rejects Jesus Christ in the life that now is. God's Word declares that there is such a heaven and it also declares that there is such a hell, and that is the only ground for believing in either, and that is a perfectly sufficient ground for believing in both.

Believe, also, its warnings as to the results in the life that now is of certain courses of action. For example, its warnings regarding the chastisement and sufferings and manifold wretchednesses of the backslider. Believe its every warning.

4. In the fourth place, *Believe its every Prophecy*. For example, believe its prophecies concerning war and peace, its prophecies concerning the future of Israel, and its many prophecies concerning the Second Coming of Christ. What the Bible so plainly prophesies concerning the Second Coming of Christ is especially

hated at present in certain at least nominally Christian quarters. This hatred of the teachings of the Bible concerning the Second Coming of Christ is blind, fanatical, bitter and fierce. It does not stop at active persecution. A well-known Professor in the Chicago University publicly advocated, during the recent war, an investigation as to whether the money that was being given for the furtherance of this precious truth did not come from German sources, and suggested that those who were teaching this truth ought to be punished as German sympathizers. A great denomination, with a glorious history, is openly making it very unpleasant, and very difficult, for any of their ministers and missionaries who hold and teach the doctrine of the Second Coming of Christ, while at the same time they welcome with open arms those who question the Virgin Birth of our Lord and the Resurrection of the body of Jesus from the dead and the reliability of the Scriptures not only into their ministry but even into their theological chairs both here in America and in China. But our part is to believe a doctrine if it is taught in the Word of God, no matter what it may cost to believe it.

II. Obey the Bible

But we should not only believe the Bible because it is the Word of God, we should also *Obey the Bible* for the same reason. The words of the Apostle James need to be earnestly heeded today, "Be ye *doers* of the Word, not hearers only, deceiving your own selves" (Jas. 1:22). As we have proved the Bible to be the

Word of God, its every commandment is God's commandment and should be obeyed. Of course, we should note carefully to whom any specific commandment is addressed. Some commandments are addressed to the Jews as Jews, some to believers in Christ, and some to individuals. The Bible always makes it clear to whom any specific commandment is addressed. Of course, every commandment to a believing Jew is also for a believing Gentile. The Bible has but one commandment for unbelievers, whether Jews or Gentiles, and that commandment is to *believe on Jesus Christ* (Jno. 6:28, 29). Until a man does that, no obedience to any other commandment in the Bible is acceptable to God. There is no use in preaching Christian ethics to unbelieving men, to men who reject Jesus Christ, to unregenerate men.

1. *Obey every Commandment of the Bible that is addressed to you.* We must not pick and choose. They are all God's Word, and to disobey any one of God's commandments is an act of rebellion against God. For example, God commands all believers in Jesus Christ to "rejoice in the Lord always" (Phil. 4:4), and for any believer in Jesus Christ to have a joyless moment is for him to disobey God. Again, God commands every believer in Jesus Christ, "In nothing be anxious" (Phil. 4:6), and for a believer in Jesus Christ to have a moment of anxiety or fear is for him to disobey God.

2. Not only obey every commandment, but *Obey exactly.* Do just what God says to do, not something

nearly like it, something that seems to you just as good, but do *exactly* what God says to do.

3. *Obey unhesitatingly.* It always pay to obey God, so when it becomes clear that God commands you in His Word to do anything, do it at once, without the slightest hesitation or questioning. Do not recoil from any commandment of God and question and parley, obey immediately.

4. *Obey gladly.* No matter how hard the commandment may seem, or what sacrifice it may involve, or what disaster seems to be involved in obedience, with joy do the very thing God tells you to do. God commands it, therefore I gladly do it. Never forget that every commandment in this Book is a commandment from your Heavenly Father, whose love to you is not only wiser than any earthly father's but more tender than any earthly mother's. You do not understand why your Father commands you to do this thing. But why should you understand? Can you not trust Him and ask no explanations? Just do it, and do it gladly.

III. Study the Bible

In the third place, we should *Study the Bible*. As the Bible is the Word of God and no other book is the Word of God, we should study it as we study no other book. Of what value is what man says, even the greatest and wisest of men, in comparison with what an infinitely wise God says? In the light of the fact that the Bible is clearly proven to be the Word of God, it is supremely irrational not to study the Bible as we study no other book.

There is in the Bible the truth that will safeguard you against every error of these times, or any times, but this truth, though it is there, will not safeguard you unless you see it and know it, and you will not see it, and cannot know it, unless you study long and earnestly the Book in which it is to be found. The Bible has no magic or "hocus-pocus" power. It has power only for the truth it contains, and to see that truth and feel its power, you must study, study, study, the Bible.

1. *Study the Bible with eagerness and avidity.* Study it with eagerness and avidity just because it is the Word of God.

2. *Study the Bible every day.* To let a single day go by without studying the Bible is to insult God. There is a deeper significance than most of us realize in the words of Acts 17:11, "Now, these were more noble than those in Thessalonica, in that they received the Word with all readiness of mind, *examining the Scriptures daily,* whether these things were so." Never let a day pass without digging into that Book. I have read the whole Book through I do not know how many times. I have read the New Testament through in Greek many, many times. I have committed whole chapters and whole books to memory. I have stored it in my heart. Nevertheless, never a day would I let pass that I did not dig into it again, not one single day. He is a wise man who so arranges his affairs as to

give a solid hour every day to Bible study. It certainly pays.

3. But not only study it every day, *Study hard.* Many do what they call "Bible study," but it is only lolling over the Bible, dreaming, mind wandering, wool gathering, instead of gathering the nuggets of gold for which one must dig and dig and dig. Give your whole mind and your whole heart to your Bible study. When you do study the Bible, *concentrate* on that one thing, roll up the sleeves of your intellect and pitch in. Mark well the significance of Solomon's words, as found in Prov. 2:1-5, "My son, if thou wilt receive my words, and lay up my commandments with thee; so as to incline thine ear unto wisdom, *and apply thy heart to understanding;* yea, if thou *cry after* discernment, and lift up thy voice for understanding; *if thou seek her as silver, and search for her as for hid treasures:* then shalt thou understand the fear of the LORD, and find the knowledge of God."

4. *Study the whole Bible;* for we have seen that the whole Bible is the Word of God, and we should seek to know the whole mind of God. We cannot afford to neglect any part of the Bible; study the Old Testament as well as the New Testament, study Matthew's Gospel and Mark's Gospel and Luke's Gospel as well as John's Gospel. Do not be content with that silly and conceited book, Kent's "Shorter Bible," or the "Shorter Bible" of anyone else. Study the *whole* Bible. Professor Kent says in the introduction to that volume of the "Shorter Bible" which appeared first, "The New Testament," that "the 'Shorter Bible'

What to Do with the Bible

aims ... to single out ... those parts of the Bible *which are of vital interest and practical value* to the present age." If these words mean anything, they certainly mean that the "Shorter Bible," while it omits much, does present everything in our present Bible, the real Bible, which is "of vital interest and practical value to the present age." That statement or implication is a gross falsehood, and not only does Kent's Bible not contain all that "is vital and of practical importance to the present age," but in what he does give he does not give what God really says, but what he thinks God would better have said, and oftentimes his alleged translation is not a translation at all, but an interpretation, and frequently a very weak and silly interpretation, and oftentimes an out-and-out substitution of his own ideas for what God really said.

How to Study, I have said elsewhere. (See "How to Study the Bible for the Greatest Profit" and "The Importance and Value of Proper Bible Study.")

IV. Memorize the Bible

In the fourth place, we should not only study the Bible, *we should commit large portions of the Bible to memory.* Fill your mind and your memory with it, and then *meditate upon it day and night.* It is as true today as when David wrote it of old, "Blessed is the man that walketh not in the counsel of the ungodly, nor standeth in the way of sinners, nor sitteth in the seat of the scornful, but his delight is in the law of the LORD; and in his law doth he *meditate day and night.* And *he* shall be like a tree planted by the rivers of water, that bringeth forth its fruit in its season, his leaf also shall not wither, and whatsoever he doeth shall prosper." (Ps. 1:1–3.) What is there in all this world that is so good to fill the memory and the heart with as the golden words of God? Happy is the man who has his memory full of them.

V. Live the Bible

In the fifth place, *Live the Bible.* I am often asked what is the best translation of the Bible—the Authorized Version, or the Revised Version, or Weymouth, or Rotherham, or Wilson's Diaglott, or Moffatt, or J. N. Darby, or what? The best translation of the Bible, beyond a question, is the translation into daily living. Get the Bible into your heart, saturate your mind with it, and then live it out. Be a walking Bible in your character and conduct, be the Word of God incarnated in a human life again today. Of course, that is only measurably possible to each one of us. It has never been fully realized in but one person, our Lord Jesus Christ, the Incarnate "Word of God." (Jno. 1:14.) The Christian is the only Bible the world reads, so be sure that you are an accurate translation into life of the written Word of God.

VI. Love the Bible

In the sixth place, *Love the Bible.* Logically, this should have come first, but there are reasons for putting it sixth. Love the Bible. The Psalmist said, "My soul breaketh for the longing that it hath unto thine ordinances at all times" (Ps. 119:20), and he said again, "The law of thy mouth is better unto me than thousands of gold and silver" (Ps. 119:72), and again, "Oh how love I thy law! It is my meditation all the day" (Ps. 119:97), and again, "I opened wide my mouth, and panted; for I longed for thy commandments" (Ps. 119:131), and again, "I rejoice at thy word, as one that findeth great spoil" (Ps. 119:162). Jeremiah says, "Thy words were found, and I did eat them; and thy words were unto me a joy and the rejoicing of my heart" (Jer. 15:16). Job said, "I have treasured up the words of his mouth more than my necessary food" (Job 23:12), and the Lord Jesus Himself said, "He that is of God hath the words of God" (Jno. 8:47). Certainly, if the Book is God's Word, and, as we have seen, it undoubtedly is, beyond an honest question, every true child of God will love and cherish it above gold. What is so precious as the revealed Will of God? That is what this Book is. Some silly people, who fancy themselves wondrous wise, talk about "Bibliolatry." I have never known a Bibliolator, that is a man who *worshiped* the Bible, but, thank God, I have known some who love the Bible, their Heavenly Father's Word, above all earthly treasures. Our Lord Jesus made two of His most wonderful promises to those who did love His Word. He says in John 14:21, "He that hath my commandments and keepeth them ("and keepeth them" means more than obeyeth them; it means to regard them and hold on to them as a precious treasure), he it is that loveth me: and he that loveth me shall be loved of my Father, and I will love him, *and will manifest myself unto him,*" and He says in Jno. 14:23, "If a man love me, he *will keep my word:* and my Father will love him, and *we will come unto him, and make our abode with him.*" Those are wonderful promises. When you get home, take them and meditate upon them. *One of the best evidences that one really is a child of God is that he really loves the Word of God.* One of the best evidences that one is not a child of God is that he does not love the Bible, that he is perfectly willing to have parts of it discredited and glad to have it cut down from its full compass to a "Shorter Bible."

VII. *Teach and Preach the Bible*

In the seventh place, *Teach and Preach the Bible.* As Paul advised Timothy, "Preach the word, be urgent in season, out of season." (2 Tim. 4:2.) What else is so worth telling people, as what God says? What other work is so important and beneficent as teaching the Word of God? Our text tells us that the Bible "completely furnishes the man of God unto every good work," because "it is profitable for teaching, for reproof, for correction, for instruction in righteousness." This Book is the one thing we must teach and preach if the people to whom we minister are to get the teaching, reproof, correction and instruction in righteousness which they so sorely need. Teach the Bible not only publicly, but from house to house (Acts 20:20), not only to crowds but to individuals, and teach and preach

What to Do with the Bible

nothing but the Bible. There is nothing else as good as the Bible to teach and preach, it "is the sword of the Spirit" (Eph. 6:17), and as David said of the sword of Goliath, "there is none like it" (1 Sam. 21:9).

I received a letter once from a Methodist pastor who was forty-five years of age. In that letter he asked me if I thought he had better take up the study of the history of Philosophy, as some of his friends were advising him to do. To this I would reply, compared with the incomparable Word of God, man's profoundest Philosophy is utter foolishness.

Every child of God can teach and preach the Bible; not necessarily to large congregations or even to Bible classes, but to individuals in the home and on the street, and everywhere. Whatever else you may be called upon to teach, Mathematics, Reading, Spelling, Grammar, Science, Philosophy, Literature, History, Latin, Greek, or whatever it may be, be sure that you also teach God's Word. They may not permit you to do it in your school but you can do it out of school. There are many ways of doing it and many places in which to do it. To sum up, Believe the Bible, for it is the Inerrant Word of God: Obey the Bible, for it is the Inerrant Word of God: Study the Bible, for it is the Inerrant Word of God: Store your Memory with the Bible, for it is the Inerrant Word of God: Live the Bible, for it is the Inerrant Word of God: Love the Bible, for it is the Inerrant Word of God: Teach and Preach the Bible, for it is the Inerrant Word of God.

CHAPTER VI

BE NOT DECEIVED: GOD IS NOT MOCKED

"Be not deceived; God is not mocked: for whatsoever a man soweth, that shall he also reap."—Gal 6:7.

I have a subject and a text tonight that I desire greatly to impress upon your minds and upon your hearts. The text and the subject are very much the same. If I can get you to follow the advice of my text and of my subject, your prosperity and your joy for time and also for eternity are assured. The subject is, "Be not Deceived; God is not mocked." The text you will find in Gal. 6:7, "Be not deceived; God is not mocked: for whatsoever a man soweth, that shall he also reap." Let these words sink into your heart, "Be not deceived; God is not mocked: for whatsoever a man soweth, that shall he also reap."

Men and women who have been defrauded by sharpers of one kind and another in this city have come to me with sad stories, sometimes heartbreaking stories, of how they have been robbed and defrauded of their all, which oftentimes with toil and pain and self-sacrificing economy they have been saving up for declining years. My blood has boiled against some men in this city, whom I could name, as I have listened to these stories. I have been able in a few instances

Be Not Deceived: God is Not Mocked

to save some poor widows and others out of the clutches of these unprincipled scoundrels. There are some men in this city I wish could be put behind prison bars where they belong. They are meaner than the common thieves and the daring bandits that our police force are now trying to stamp out. But I have especially in mind tonight a gang of crooks that is the most dangerous gang in all the world and they are operating here at the present time. The head of the gang, who keeps himself out of sight, would like to kill me and every man who is trying to expose him, if he could. And he would succeed in killing me only God protects me, and "If God be for us, who can be against us?" (Rom. 8:31). Who this Gang are, and who the Head of the Gang, who keeps under cover and tries to hide his identity, is, will develop as we go on.

I. The World's History is a History of Deception

The first thing I have to call your attention to tonight is, that the history of this old world in which you and I live has been a history of deception from its very beginning to the present day. The first man and woman who ever lived upon this earth were deceived, deceived by the Devil, and they lost Eden, and were driven out of that matchlessly beautiful home to earn their bread by the sweat of their brow amid thorns and briars and sickness and death, and they would have been lost eternally had not God stepped in with His mercy and grace and pardoning love. They were deceived by the Devil. *He got them to be-*

lieve that God's Word was not true, to believe his word rather than God's Word, to believe that God's Word was not inspired and literally true, that it did not mean exactly what it said; and so they lost all. Well, it has gone on that way from that day to this; only it has grown worse, far worse in recent days. The Devil has tried to deceive every man that has lived on the face of this earth and he has succeeded pretty well with most of us, and in just so far as he has succeeded there has been sorrow and pain and loss and anguish; and oftentimes, when men's eyes have not been opened in time, eternal ruin. There is not a man or woman here tonight who has not at some time in their life been the victim of the Devil's deception, and how we have suffered by it.

1. How often *the Devil has persuaded us that we could do wrong and gain something by it.* We knew better and yet somehow we let Satan pull the wool over our eyes and we did the wrong act; and how bitterly we have repented of it, how we have suffered for it, what would we not give if we could take that wrong act back and undo the mischief we have done.

I remember a young man I met one night in an after-meeting. He was almost in despair. He had been walking the streets of a great city. He had been tempted to do wrong. He knew better. But the Devil deceived him, and he scarcely stopped to think and before he came to himself the act was done, and then the enormity of it came before him. He thought of his mother, he thought of the lovely girl in another city to whom he was engaged, he thought of God, for he was a professing Christian; and he was crushed. It was awful to see the way that fine young fellow suffered, suffered because he had allowed himself to be deceived. The way some men and women have sobbed as they have told me how they had been robbed of everything by land sharks and crooks of one kind and another in this city, was nothing to the way that brokenhearted young man sobbed because he had let the Devil deceive him and lead him into that awful sin.

I remember a young woman who allowed the Devil and one of his representatives in the form of a goodlooking and gifted but unprincipled man to deceive her. She too did not stop to think until the deed was done; and then she did think and she was almost crazed with shame. And then the Devil stepped in again and said to her, "there is no remedy"—and that was a worse lie than the first one, for there was a remedy in the pardoning love of God and the atoning and cleansing blood of Jesus Christ. But the Devil said, "there is no remedy," and the poor girl believed him and sent a bullet whizzing through her maddened brain and sent herself to hell to spend eternity with the scoundrel who had deceived her.

One of the things that impresses me most as I move about from city to city and watch what is going on and as I listen to the stories of sin and sorrow that people come to me to pour into my ears, and as I read the papers is, how easily men and women are deceived by their fellow men and how easily they are deceived by the Devil. I ask many a man and woman who come to me and tell of their folly and its consequences, "How could you have done it? Why didn't you know better?" And they shake their heads and say, "I don't know. I don't understand it myself. I did know better. I was deceived." Oh let us ask God to keep His Words ringing in our hearts day and night "Be not deceived," "*Be not deceived,*" "*Be Not Deceived.*" There is many and many a man in this house tonight who knows as he listens to my words that he is being deceived. There is many a woman here tonight who knows she is being deceived, being deceived by the great arch enemy of our souls, being deceived by the Devil, being deceived to your present misery and to your eternal ruin. Why then do you allow yourself to be deceived? Why do you continue to allow yourself to be deceived? Do you not know what the final end is? It is hell and everlasting hell unless you wake up and repent.

"Oh," some of you say, "I do not believe there is any Devil." Well that is where you are being deceived the very worst way. The apostle Peter knew what he was talking about when he said, "Your adversary *the devil,* as a roaring lion, walketh about, seeking whom he may devour." (1 Pet. 5:8.) And there is not anyone of whom he makes a quicker meal than the one who thinks "there isn't any lion around." The apostle Paul knew what he was talking about when he wrote, "Put on the whole armour of God, that ye may be able to stand against the wiles of *the devil.* For our wrestling is not against flesh and blood, but against the principalities, against the powers, against the world-rulers of this darkness, against the spiritual hosts of wickedness in the heavenly places." (Eph.

6:11,12.) And there is no one the Devil gets a better strangle hold upon and downs quicker than the one who thinks there is no Devil to wrestle with. The Lord Jesus Christ knew what he was talking about when he taught us to pray to our Father in heaven to "deliver us from *the Evil one*" (Matt. 6:13 R. V.). "Be not deceived," young man. "Be not deceived," young woman.

2. *The Devil not only deceives us by persuading us that we can do wrong and gain something by it, but he deceives us by persuading us that certain things are not wrong, that in our inmost hearts we know are wrong.*

How many young people there are tonight, people of decent parentage at that, who have been led in the last twelve months here in Los Angeles to do things that they once abhorred and that every really decent man and woman abhors still. Some of you are here tonight. Do not get up and go out or you will expose yourself to everyone here. You do not wish to do that and I certainly do not wish you to. Just sit still and listen. Do not giggle, either, for nothing gives a guilty man or woman away so quickly as a guilty giggle. Why do you now do these awful things you once so wisely abhorred? I will tell you why. It is because the Devil whispers, "there is no harm in it. It is all right. You are an old fogy puritan to fancy it is wrong," or he says, "Well, the circumstances in your case are very peculiar. Of course it would be wrong under ordinary circumstances but not in your circumstances." And you suffer the voice of conscience and the voice of God's Word and the voice of the Holy Spirit, yes and the voice of self-respect and the voice of common decency to be silenced and you do the foul and wicked thing, and then you wake up to the horror of what you have done; or it may be, worse yet, you now set your heart in sin and go on and on and on and on—whither? into Hell.

If I could only tell you what a broken-hearted mother told me only three Sunday nights ago right here in this auditorium as to what her daughter had said to her in trying to explain her shocking conduct, many of you would be startled and shocked. And some of you would have to say, "Yes that is my case too." Oh, the way the Devil is deceiving a multitude of young men and young women in our city is appalling.

How many the Devil is deceiving today by saying, "There is nothing wrong in a glass of wine"; "There is nothing wrong in being free with persons of the opposite sex"; there is nothing wrong in going to see the movies that are full of impure suggestions; there is nothing wrong in dances, of a character that a few years ago would not have been tolerated except among professionally bad women and morally rotten men; there is nothing wrong in games that lead straight to the gaming table and a gambler's ruin; there is nothing wrong in using the Lord's Day for pleasure-seeking and to the neglect of that never-dying soul that you are educating for an eternal heaven or for an eternal hell." There is nothing wrong in the one thousand and one things that in your best moments you see are gateways to hell. "Be Not Deceived." How these startling and arousing words of God need to be emphasized and dinned into the ears of a multitude of foolish men and women in our day, "Be not deceived."

II. We Cannot Mock God

At the foundation of all of Satan's deceptions is the thought that we can mock God, that we can turn up our noses at God (that is the exact force of the word translated "mocked" in our text), that we can sneer at God, that we can deride God, that we can get the laugh on God, that we can deceive God, *that we can treat God and His Word and His laws with contempt,* and yet prosper. It is a blasphemous, an outrageously blasphemous thought. But many of you here entertain it, though you probably have never put it into words; but you are acting on that foolish, wicked thought every day that you live, the thought that you can somehow outwit God.

When for example anyone fancies that he can do wrong and gain anything by it, he is trying to mock God, he is turning up his nose at God. "Be not deceived; *God is not mocked.*" Men disobey God and yet seem to prosper; but wait, just wait. God is never in a hurry but God always gains the day. Men and women, if there is any point upon which you cannot afford to be deceived, it is this: You cannot mock God, you cannot overreach God, you cannot deceive God, you cannot get the best of God. *The biggeset fool in the universe is the man who thinks he can fool God.* Yet there are many fools of that sort. There are many in this house tonight.

Is the Bible the Inerrant Word of God?

Let us consider some of those who are trying to mock God, to deceive God, to get the best of God, to turn up their nose at God.

1. First of all, *the man who thinks he can do wrong and gain by it is trying to mock God, to get the best of God.* God is a God of infinite holiness, perfect justice and inviolable law. And it is God's inviolable law that whoever sins shall suffer, "whatsoever a man soweth, that shall he also reap." From the creation of this world down to the present day there has never been one single sin that paid, not one. There has never been one single sin small or great that did not bring loss to the sinner. The law that whosoever puts his hand into the fire shall get burned is not so sure and inexorable as the law that whosoever sins must suffer. Young man you are contemplating a sin tonight; commit it, and you will pay the penalty, you cannot escape it. There is not power enough on earth or in hell to protect any sinner from suffering loss by his own sin, and by his every sin. You can escape some human courts. No man or woman or angel or devil can escape the penalty of God's every day court of inexorable justice that sees to it that every sinner, great or small, rich or poor, pays an adequate penalty for every sin he commits. It is as certain that every sin any man or woman commits shall cost the sinner an adequate penalty of loss and suffering of one kind or another as that a stone dropped from a height will fall toward the earth. Perhaps in an hour, perhaps in a week, perhaps in a year, perhaps not for years, but sooner or later you will pay for every sin you

commit. Now if in the light of that absolutely certain fact you commit the sin that you are contemplating tonight, you are a hopeless fool. "Be not deceived; God is not mocked: for whatsoever a man soweth, that shall he also reap."

2. In the second place: *The man or woman who tries to hide from God the sin which they have already committed is trying to mock God.* You cannot do it. "Be sure your sin will find you out" (Num. 32:23). Men may not find you out, but God will. He sees the sin: you cannot hide it from Him. It is not only written in God's Book; it is also written in universal experience, "He that covereth his sins shall not prosper" (Prov. 28:13). The sinner may hide his sin from the eye of man but he cannot hide it from the all-seeing eye of God. Therefore, every sin brings with it in due time its proper harvest. Do you wish to know the secret of the failure and the wretchedness in your life? I will tell you. The sin you are trying to hide from God.

How well King David seemed to cover up his sin. The only man who would know of it and would call him to account for it was dead and buried; and King David thought that the knowledge of his sin was buried too and that he could rest easy now. But no! God knew of the sin and David knew of the sin; and there was no rest for him, no indeed, only utter wretchedness in his heart. David wrote the story of it in later life. He said, "When I kept silence, my bones waxed old through my roaring all the day long. For day and night Thy hand was heavy upon me: my moisture was changed as with the drought of summer" (Ps. 32:3, 4).

I know a woman who had sinned and she succeeded in hiding her sin from every human eye. No one knew it, not one; only she herself AND GOD. It haunted her, it hunted her, it drove her from place to place, from city to city, from land to land. It caused her years and years of agony, nearly fifteen years in all, fifteen years of hell on earth, until she confessed it to me and to God and believed on the Lord Jesus Christ, and found full pardon and perfect peace. "Be not deceived; God is not mocked."

3. In the third place; *Men think that they can mock God, that they can sneer at God, that they can outwit God, that they can circumvent God, that they can turn up their nose at God, by questioning or denying or ridiculing His Word.* Quote the Bible to some men, read God's commandments and God's warnings against sin and what God says about judgment and eternity to some men and they will laugh at it and at you. But listen, "God is not mocked." Pharaoh did the same thing. When Moses declared the Word of Jehovah to him he replied, "Who is Jehovah that I should hearken unto his voice and let Israel go? I know not Jehovah and moreover I will not let Israel go." But Pharaoh found out who Jehovah was, and he also found out that God's Word was sure. God kept every word of warning. And you too may laugh at God's Word and sneer at the one who believes in verbal inspiration and the literal accuracy of the Word of God; you may laugh at the stern warnings of this

Be Not Deceived: God is Not Mocked

book as to the eternal destruction of the one who rejects Jesus Christ or refuses to confess Him before the world, but *you too will find out who the God of the Bible is, and you will find out that every word in this Book is true and every warning sure.* If you do not find it out in the life that now is you will find it out in Hell; find it out when it is too late to repent.

The men before the flood ridiculed the warnings God gave through Noah. They laughed at the Word of God. But God was not mocked. He kept His Word to the letter. The flood came and carried them all away.

The sons-in-law of Lot down in Sodom laughed at God's Word. God's warnings through Lot to his sons-in-law seemed as idle tales ("folklore" our "modern scholars" would call them). God's warnings seemed to them a huge joke, just as the warnings of God do today to many a hardened sinner and many a boastful infidel and many a "liberal preacher." But Lot's sons-in-law found out God was not mocked. God kept His Word. Sodom was destroyed and Lot's sons-in-law in it and with it.

The Jews of Jeremiah's time mocked at God's Word. They ridiculed the warnings of God's faithful messenger, Jeremiah. All their "leading scholars" scoffed at the predictions that God made through Jeremiah. False prophets arose and preached a "more liberal" and a pleasanter and "more philosophical" theology. They told the people that Jerusalem would not be taken and destroyed. They were "the scholarly men" and "the leading theologians" of the day and the mass of the people believed them and laughed at God's Word and at His faithful messenger. *But God was not mocked.* History tells us that God kept His word, that Jerusalem was destroyed and sacked, that King Zedekiah was taken, and his sons were slain before his eyes and that then his own eyes were put out, *all just as God had said it would be.* It all came out just as God by His servant Jeremiah had said it would. God's "historical interpretation" of His own Word was an exactly "literal interpretation."

The men of our Lord Jesus Christ's own time ridiculed the Word of God as spoken by our Lord Himself. They scoffed at the idea that judgment would come upon the apostate nation, that Jerusalem and the temple would be destroyed, and that they should perish miserably. Yes, they scoffed at all His loving but stern words and they nailed our Lord Himself to the cross for making them in His great love for them. The voice of warning was hushed in death,—but "God was not mocked." God kept His word to the very letter. History outside of the Bible tells us that God kept His word with fearful thoroughness and "literality." Jerusalem was surrounded by the armies of Rome just as Jesus Christ said it would be. Jerusalem and the magnificent temple were razed to the ground just as God through Jesus Christ said it would be. Starvation stalked the streets and the streets ran with blood in the most awful siege of all human history, just as God through the Lord Jesus Christ said it would be. More than a million people perished in that siege and the Jewish leaders hung on crosses in the hills around

Be Not Deceived: God is Not Mocked

about the city. No, God was not mocked. They reaped what they had sown. "Be not deceived; God is not mocked; for whatsoever a man soweth, that shall he also reap." Oh, you men who call yourselves skeptics and infidels and "advanced scholars" and "New Theology" men and "Modernists," you men who question this Book and question and deny and even ridicule its warnings of coming doom, "Be not deceived; God is not mocked." History proves it. God's Word has been questioned over and over again. Very specious arguments have been brought against it over and over again. Men of influence and brains and eloquence have derided it, over and over again. All so-called "Scholarship" has been against it over and over again. But God's Word has never failed; and it never will. Every word of God regarding judgment upon individuals and upon nations up to the present moment has been kept, kept to the last letter. And do you think God will not keep His word in times yet to come concerning those who reject Jesus Christ today to the last letter? He kept His word about Tyre. He kept His word about Babylon. He kept His word about Nineveh. He kept His word about Jerusalem. He kept His word about Greece. He kept His word about Persia. He kept His word about the Roman Empire. He kept His word about the Jew. Look into the Bible and see what God says and then look into history and see what history tells us God has done; and you will find that *the Bible and History exactly match.* God has kept His word, His word as found in this book, about all these nations, and will He not keep His word regarding us? What is His word regarding us? Listen, "The Lord Jesus shall be revealed from heaven with the angels of his power in flaming fire, rendering vengeance to *them that know not God,* and to *them that obey not the gospel of our Lord Jesus; who shall suffer punishment, even eternal destruction from the face of the Lord and from the glory of His might"* (2 Thess. 1:7–9). That is God's word. Do you doubt whether God will keep it? "Be not deceived; God is not mocked: for whatsoever a man soweth, that shall he also reap."

What then shall we do? In the light of these plain statements of God's Word and these undeniable facts of history demonstrating the absolute certainty and Inerrancy and literal accuracy of God's Word there is only one thing for any really intelligent man or woman to do. That is to accept Jesus Christ as your personal Savior at once. Surrender absolutely to Him as your Lord and Master at once. Begin to confess Him as your Lord before the world at once. Who will do it now?

CHAPTER VII

IS IT ABSOLUTELY CERTAIN THAT THE BODY OF JESUS THAT WAS NAILED TO THE CROSS, THAT REALLY DIED, AND THAT WAS LAID IN JOSEPH'S TOMB, WAS RAISED FROM THE DEAD?

"Remember Jesus Christ, *risen from the dead,* of the seed of David, *according to my gospel.*"—2 Tim. 2:8.
"Now *I make known unto you, brethren, the gospel which I preached* unto you, which also ye received, wherein also ye stand. . . . For I delivered unto you first of all that which I also received: *that Christ died* for our sins according to the scriptures; and *that he was buried;* and *that he hath been raised on the third day* according to the scriptures and *that he appeared (was seen) to Cephas;* then *to the twelve;* then *he appeared (was seen) to above five hundred brethren at once,* of whom the greater part remain until now, but some are fallen asleep; then *he appeared (was seen) to James;* then *to all the apostles;* and *last of all,* as to a child untimely born he appeared (was seen) *to me* also. . . . (14) And *if Christ hath not been raised,* then is *our preaching vain,* your *faith also is vain. Yea, and we are found false witnesses of God;* because *we witnessed of God that He raised up Christ:* whom he raised not up, if so be that the dead are not raised. For if the dead are not raised, neither hath Christ been raised; and *if Christ hath not been raised,* your *faith is vain; ye are yet in your sins.* Then they also which have fallen asleep in Christ have perished. . . . (20) But now hath Christ *been raised from the dead,* the first fruits of them that are asleep."—1 Cor. 15:1, 3-9, 14-18, 20.

"And as they were affrighted, and bowed down their faces to the earth, they said unto them, Why seek ye the living among the dead? *He is not here, but is risen:* remember how he spake unto you when he was yet in Galilee, saying that the Son of man must be delivered up into the hands of sinful men, and *be crucified,* and *the third day rise again.*"—Luke 24: 5-7.

"And entering into the tomb, they saw a young man sitting on the right side, arrayed in a white robe; and they were amazed. And he saith unto them, Be not amazed: ye seek *Jesus, the Nazarene, which hath been crucified:* he *is risen; he is not here: behold, the place where they laid him!*"—Mark 16: 5, 6.

Christians throughout the world are celebrating today the Resurrection of Jesus Christ from the Dead. Everybody who has any right whatever to call himself a Christian, and every man who has any intellectual honesty who does call himself a Christian, believes in some sort of a Resurrection of our Lord Jesus. But the Resurrection of Jesus that many who call themselves Christians believe in in this peculiar day in which we are living is not any such resurrection as is plainly set forth in the Four Gospels, in the Acts of the Apostles and in the fifteenth chapter of First Corinthians. One prominent teacher on the Foregin Mission field, who calls himself a Christian, and who has many followers, teaches that the Resurrection of Jesus was simply the continuation in others of the spirit, and life, and principles of Jesus, that He lives again in those who represent Him and and carry on His teaching and work today. This I think is an extreme case, but there are many others, including not a few supposedly orthodox ministers and theological professors here in America and in England, as well as numerous teachers in missionary schools and colleges in China and other missionary lands, who do not go as far as this view of the Resurrection of Jesus just described, but who do deny the Resurrection of the very body that was nailed to the cross and laid in Joseph's tomb. They say that they believe in the Resurrection of Jesus, but not in the Resurrection of the body of the Lord Jesus, but in a spiritual Resurrection. Some who will today celebrate the Resurrection of Jesus will celebrate in their hearts (and some will even say so openly) not a Resurrection of the Body of our Lord, the Body that was nailed to the cross and taken down from the cross by loving hands and laid in Joseph's tomb, and that the women who came early on the first Easter morning to embalm it found gone, but the Resurrection of the spirit of Jesus. Professor Harris Franklin Rall, President and Professor of Systematic Theology in the Iliff School of Theology, Denver, Colorado, in his book entitled "New Testament History, A Study of the Beginnings of Christianity," seemingly seeks to discredit the accounts of His Resurrection given in the Four Gospels. He says on page one hundred and forty, "It may be stated at the very first that *only by violence can these accounts be harmonized* in important details. When we come to a closer study of these records, (*i. e.*, the Gospel records of the Resurrection of Jesus Christ) we are met by two questions. How are we to reconcile the apparent differences in these accounts; and, how are we to conceive the manner of the Resurrection and of these appearances?" This statement of Professor Rall, Ph.D., that the Gospel accounts can be "harmonized in important details" "only by violence," is, as every thorough student of the Bible knows, absolutely without warrant in the facts in the case. Shortly afterwards he goes on to say, *"There have been differences of interpretation* likewise *as to the manner of the Resurrection and the appearances.* Our oldest witness, Paul, *lays no stress upon the physical."* We shall show later that this statement is absolutely untrue, that Paul lays tremendous "stress upon the physical." Professor Rall admits that (to use his own words), "Luke on the other hand emphasizes the physical even to the extent of picturing Jesus as eating" (Luke 24:39-43). Professor Rall seems to have forgotten that Luke was the companion of Paul, and that Luke's Gospel is the distinctively Pauline Gospel. There then follows in Professor Rall's book a frank statement by him that there are discrepancies in the accounts, with the plain implication that the accounts are not accurate or to be depended upon. Then he says, *"Nor is it important* to answer the second question (that is, the question as to 'the manner of the Resurrection')". We shall see before we get through that the question of "the manner of the Resurrection of Jesus" is of the very highest importance. Professor Rall's whole object, apparently, is to discredit the Resurrection of the Body of Jesus. Indeed, he says in the immediately following sentence, "The actual issue is whether we believe in the reality of the spiritual world" (page 141). We shall see that this is not the issue at all, but that the issue is, shall we believe in the Resurrection of Jesus Christ as it is set forth in the Bible. Professor Rall closes this paragraph by saying, "The *one* clear fact, without which the wonderful story of early Christianity is a

Was the Body of Jesus Raised From the Dead?

mere riddle, is the fact that these disciples were following a *living Lord,* and not a dead and defeated leader." Now this is not *"the one* clear fact." *We shall see that the one clear fact is, that they "were following a Lord" who was not only "living" but whose body had been raised from the dead,* not whose *spirit* had been raised from the dead, but whose *Body* had been raised from the dead. But this teaching of President and Professor Rall, Ph.D., is characteristic of a good deal of the shallow nonsense and utterly heretical teaching regarding the Resurrection of Jesus Christ our Lord that exists today not only in the Methodist Episcopal church, in which Professor Rall is so prominent a leader, but in other orthodox churches as well. Professor Rall's prominence in the Methodist Episcopal Church is seen by the fact that two of his books, including the one from which I have just quoted, are included in the course of study that the Bishops of the Methodist Episcopal Church require to be read in the prescribed course of study by every candidate for the ministry in the Methodist Episcopal Church.

So the vital question *today* is not merely, Do you believe in the Resurrection of the Lord Jesus Christ? But, Do you believe in the Resurrection *of the Body* of the Lord Jesus Christ? Do you believe in a *real* Resurrection? Do you believe that the very Body of Jesus that was nailed to the Cross of Calvary and that really died, and that was laid in Joseph's tomb and that was gone from the tomb when Mary and her companions visited the tomb, and when John and Peter visited the tomb, on the first Easter morning, do you believe that body was raised from the dead and transformed into the glorious body the Lord Jesus now inhabits in the Glory?

So my subject this morning is: *Is It Absolutely Certain That the Body of Jesus That Was Nailed to the Cross, That Really Died, and That Was Taken Down and Laid in Joseph's Tomb, Was Raised from the Dead?* I have four texts. The first is, 2 Tim. 2:8, "Remember Jesus Christ, *risen from the dead, of the seed of David, according to my gospel.*" The second is, 1 Cor. 15:1, 3–9, 14–18, 20, "Now *I make known unto you, brethren, the gospel which I preached unto you,* which also ye received, wherein also ye stand. . . . (3) For *I delivered unto you first of all* that which I also received: *that Christ died for our sins* according to the scriptures; and *that he was buried;* and *that he hath been raised on the third day* according to the scriptures; and *that he appeared (was seen) to Cephas;* then *to the twelve;* then he *appeared (was seen) to above five hundred brethren at once, of whom the greater part remain until now,* but some are fallen asleep; then he appeared (was seen) to James; then to all the apostles; and last of all, as to a child untimely born he appeared (was seen) to me also. . . . (14) And *if Christ hath not been raised,* then is *our preaching vain,* your *faith also is vain.* Yea, and *we are found false witness of God;* because *we witnessed of God that He raised up Christ;* whom he raised not up, if *so be that the dead are not raised.* For if the dead are not raised, neither hath Christ been raised; and *if Christ hath not been raised, your faith is vain; ye are yet in your sins.* Then they also which have fallen asleep in Christ have perished. . . . (20) *But now hath Christ been raised from the dead,* the first fruits of them that are asleep." My third text is, Luke 24:5–7, "And as they were affrighted, and bowed down their faces to the earth, they said unto them, Why seek ye the living among the dead? *He is not here, but is risen:* remember how he spake unto you when he was yet in Galilee, saying that the Son of man must be delivered up into the hands of sinful men, and *be crucified,* and *the third day rise again."* My fourth text is Mark 16:5, 6, "And entering into the tomb, they saw a young man sitting on the right side, arrayed in a white robe; and they were amazed. And he saith unto them, Be not amazed: *ye seek Jesus, the Nazarene, which hath been crucified: he is risen, he is not here:* behold, *the place where they laid him!"*

I. A Merely Spiritual Resurrection of Jesus No Resurrection at All

Let me say at the very outset of our study of this fundamentally important question that a merely spiritual Resurrection of Jesus, the Christ of God, a resurrection of His spirit but not a resurrection of His body, is a mere travesty of the Resurrection set forth so plainly in each one of the Four Gospels, and in the Acts of the Apostles and in the fifteenth chapter of First Corinthians. This is clearly seen from the four texts I have just quoted and is also seen from a careful study of exactly what the Four Gospels and the

Acts of the Apostles say in various places, and from anything approaching a careful study of the fifteenth chapter of First Corinthians. Indeed, a *Resurrection of the Spirit of Jesus but not of His Body, is in reality no resurrection at all.* It was His body that died. His spirit never died, and, of course, therefore, could never have been raised. Peter says distinctly in 1 Pet. 3:18, "Because Christ also suffered for sins once, the righteous for the unrighteous, that he might bring us to God; *being put to death in the flesh* but *made alive in the spirit."* These words distinctly teach us that it was the flesh, *i. e.,* the body, that was put to death, but that while the body was dead the living spirit of Jesus went into Hades, as we read in the next verse "in which (that is in the spirit) also he went and preached unto the spirits in prison."

The spirit of Jesus was not laid in Joseph's tomb. Peter in his wonderful sermon on the day of Pentecost plainly declares in Acts 2:29–32, "Brethren, I may say unto you freely of the patriarch David, that he both died and was buried, and his tomb is with us unto this day. Being therefore a prophet, and knowing that God had sworn with an oath to him, that of the fruit of his loins he would set one upon his throne, he foreseeing this spake of *the resurrection of the Christ,* that neither was He left in *Hades,* nor did *His flesh* see corruption. This Jesus did God raise up, *whereof we all are witnesses."* Now Peter here says that "He," *i. e.,* Jesus Himself, His spirit, went into *"Hades,"* but that *"His flesh,"* that is, His body, which was all that lay in Joseph's tomb, was *preserved from corruption."*

Furthermore, Jesus Himself declared in Matt. 12:40 that during the three days and the three nights that His body would be in Joseph's tomb that the "Son of man, *i. e., He Himself, would be "in the heart of the earth," that is, in Hades.*

Further still, Jesus declared to the penitent thief hanging upon a cross by His side that, though His body would lie in Joseph's tomb, He Himself, His real self, His spirit, would *that very day* accompany the dying thief into "Paradise," *i. e.*, into that part of Hades into which the spirits of the righteous dead went at death (up to the time of the Ascension of the Lord Jesus). (Luke 23:39–43, especially v. 43.)

Countless different lines of proof converge to this one point, that the Resurrection of Jesus was a Resurrection of His body and that a merely Spiritual Resurrection of Jesus, *i. e.*, a Resurrection of His Spirit only and not of His very Body is no Resurrection at all.

II. *The Resurrection of the Spirit of Jesus but Not a Resurrection of His Body is a Dream without One Vestige of Historical or Other Proof*

Not only is *a Resurrection of the spirit of Jesus* (*but not a Resurrection of His Body*) no Resurrection at all, furthermore *it is only a dream, i. e., it is something of which there is no historical proof whatever, or evidence of any kind.* Read any one of the four accounts of the Resurrection of Christ in any one of the Four Gospels and, if you are honestly seeking to find out what these Four Gospels really describe and not catching for straws of evidence to support a mere manmade theory (or pipe-dream), you cannot avoid seeing that each one of the Four Gospels describes a Resurrection, and a disappearance from Joseph's tomb, *of the body* of Jesus, and *an appearance (visible seeing) of this same body of Jesus* to various disciples and groups of disciples. The same thing is true of the descriptions of the Resurrection of Jesus given in various chapters in the Acts of the Apostles, and the same thing is also beyond a question true of Paul's account of the Resurrection of Jesus given in First Corinthians fifteen.

These so-called "scholarly" men who seek to discredit a Resurrection of the body of Jesus and to teach a Resurrection of the spirit of Jesus, and who claim to be exponents of a "scientific method" of Bible study, and who pose as "advanced thinkers," are in real fact so utterly unscientific in their methods of thinking and reasoning as to believe in a Resurrection of Jesus of such a character that there is not one smallest shred of historic evidence for it, nor one word of reliable testimony for it, nor one particle of any evidence of any kind whatever. *Every particle of historical evidence and of testimony (and of evidence of any kind) of a Resurrection of Jesus, concerns a Resurrection of the body of Jesus. If there was not a Resurrection of the body of Jesus, there was no Resurrection at all.* There is no escaping this. If the body of Jesus was not raised from the dead, if the body that was nailed to the cross and died and was taken down and laid in Joseph's tomb was not raised from the dead and passed out of the tomb, then every statement in the Four Gospels concerning the Resurrection of Jesus is a deliberate fraud, and Peter and Paul were conscienceless liars and Christianity as a whole is the most stupendous fraud and humbug ever foisted on the human race by unscrupulous men.

On the other hand, any man who believes in the Resurrection of the Body of Jesus, the very body that was nailed to the cross and died, and that was taken down and laid in Joseph's tomb, is believing something for which the external historical evidence and the internal evidence and the circumstantial evidence is overwhelmingly conclusive. The men who believe in a spiritual Resurrection of Jesus, but not in the Resurrection of His body, are utterly and ludicrously unscientific: the men who believe in the Resurrection of the very body of Jesus that was nailed to the cross and died, and was taken down and laid in Joseph's tomb, and that was gone when the women and others visited the tomb on the first Easter morning, are thoroughly "scientific" in that they hold a theory that is built upon the exact facts in the case, and they, beyond an honest question, are absolutely correct in their position.

The question of our subject, "Is it absolutely certain that the body of Jesus that was nailed to the cross, that really died, and that was laid in Joseph's tomb, was raised from the dead," is therefore one of immeasurable importance. The truth or falsity of the whole Christian Religion depends upon the answer to this question. Paul says, and says rightly, in 1 Cor. 15:14,

15, *"And if Christ hath not been raised,* then is our preaching vain, your faith also is vain. Yea, and *we are found false witnesses of God;* because *we witnessed of God that he raised up Christ:* whom he raised not up, if so be that the dead are not raised." And he goes still further in the four following verses and says, "For if the dead are not raised, neither hath Christ been raised: and *if Christ hath not been raised, your faith is vain;* ye are *yet in your sins.* Then they also which are fallen asleep in Christ *have perished.* If we have only hoped in Christ in this life we are of all men most pitiable." If the Resurrection of the body of Jesus from the dead is a historic certainty, then Christianity with all its distinctive doctrines and all its predictions and all its promises and all its blessings stands; it rests upon the absolutely unshakable foundation of proven fact. But, if it cannot be proven that the body of Jesus Christ was raised from the dead, then Christianity falls to the ground in complete and utter ruin, and every distinctive doctrine of Christianity vanishes and all its hopes are a mirage. Thank God! it is possible to prove to a demonstration that the body of Jesus, the very body that was nailed to the cross, the very body that was "crucified" (Mark 16:6) and actually "died," the very body from whose pierced side the water and the blood were seen to flow, the very body that lay three nights and three days in Joseph's tomb, that that very body was raised and transformed and glorified. I am as certain that the dead body of Jesus was raised from the dead as I am that I stand here; and before I close I expect to make every man

Was the Body of Jesus Raised From the Dead?
and woman in this audience *who really wants to know the truth and is willing to obey the truth* just as certain about it as I am.

III. The Body of Jesus Christ Was Really Dead

The first thing to prove is that the body of Jesus was really dead, when it was taken down from the cross. There was a large company of scholars some years ago who did not wish to believe in the Resurrection of the body of Jesus Christ but who were not able to escape the force of the fact, which all students have been compelled to admit, that the disciples believed that Jesus had risen, that the tomb was found empty, and that at least some of their company had seen Him alive after His crucifixion and supposed death. So they invented the theory that the body of Jesus was not really dead when it was taken down from the cross but in a "swoon" and that it was worked over and brought back to conscious life, and that therefore the alleged Resurrection of the body of Jesus was not in reality a case of Resurrection but of resuscitation. The great German scholar Heinrich Eberhard Gottlob Paulus (1761–1851) was the leading exponent of this theory, if not its author. This same theory has been revived and is being urged again in recent days by many (including distinguished scholars) who are unwilling to admit the supernatural and therefore are unwilling to admit the reality of the Resurrection of the *Body of Jesus*. But there is a passage in one of the accounts of the Resurrection that utterly annihilates this theory,

It is Jno. 19:31–34, "The Jews therefore, because of the Preparation, that the bodies should not remain on the cross upon the Sabbath (for the day of that Sabbath was a high day—it was the yearly Passover Sabbath, not the weekly Sabbath, Saturday) asked of Pilate that their legs might be broken, and that they might be taken away. The soldiers therefore came, and brake the legs of the first, and of the other that was crucified with Him: but when they came to Jesus, and saw that he was dead already, they brake not his legs: howbeit one of the soldiers with a spear pierced his side, and *straightway there came out blood and water.*" What I wish you to note here is John's statement that "blood and water" came out from the "pierced" side of Jesus. This statement of John's proves two things. First, it proves the genuineness and minute accuracy of the story as here recorded: second, it proves that Jesus was really dead. While John tells us that he "saw" "blood and water" flow out he does not tell us why "blood and water" flowed out. Why does not John explain that to us? Simply because he did not know the explanation himself. There was not a man on earth at that time, nor for sixteen centuries at least, that knew the explanation of that fact. The physiological explanation was entirely unknown to John or anyone else at that time. The explanation is this. The Lord Jesus died of "extravasation of the blood," or, what is commonly known as, "a broken heart," just as it was predicted in the sixty-ninth Psalm and the twentieth verse that He would die. What occurs when one dies of a broken heart? The one who dies in this way throws out his arms (of course Jesus' arms were already stretched out on and nailed to the Cross), utters a loud cry (Jesus cried, "My God, My God, why hast Thou forsaken Me?"), the blood flows from the ruptured heart into the pericardium, the sac surrounding the heart. There the blood stands for a short time, and then separates into its constituent parts, serum (or, water) and clot (or red corpuscles or blood). When the soldier pierced the pericardium with his spear the blood and water there gathered flowed out. This is the scientific explanation of the recorded fact, but John did not know this explanation. As we have already said, no one then living knew it, no one knew it for centuries afterwards. Is it conceivable that a writer in fabricating an account of events that never occurred should have made up and put into that account an apparently insignificant fact that has a strict scientific explanation, fitting in minutest detail into the various facts recorded, but an explanation which neither he nor anyone living on the earth at the time could possibly have known? Of course, it is an absolute impossibility, and it demonstrates the exact and minute truthfulness of the record, and, furthermore, it utterly annihilates "the swoon theory." There can be no doubt that Jesus was really dead and the theory that He was merely in a swoon and not dead, and that the supposed Resurrection was not a Resurrection at all but merely a resuscitation collapses.

When I was holding in the leading cities of England my noon meetings for business and professional men, in which I presented the evidences of the Resurrection of Jesus Christ, the most persistent and one of the most gifted opponents of the truth was Mr. Blatchford, perhaps the leading aggressive rationalist of the day in England. Mr. Blatchford came out in a publication in which he attempted to show that the body of Jesus was not raised from the dead, and advocated "the swoon theory." One of the main points in his argument was that when the side of Jesus was pierced, the body bled, and he asked the seemingly pertinent question, "Does a dead man bleed?" At first glance, it seemed like a good point, but on more careful study it is evident that if Blatchford had known a little more about physiology, and had been candid, he would not have used this argument; for while it is true that a man who dies under ordinary circumstances does not bleed after he is dead, if *a man dies of a broken heart*, the blood, as we have already seen, flows into the pericardium and there separates into its constituent parts of serum (or, water) and clot (red blood corpuscles or blood), and if some time after his death the side is pierced and the spear enters the pericardium and is drawn out, blood and water will flow out, not proving that he is not dead but proving that he died in a peculiar way, of a broken heart. So Blatchford's argument is a boomerang, and so far from proving that Jesus was not dead, proves that He was dead, and dead of a broken heart.

Was the Body of Jesus Raised From the Dead?

IV. The Proof that the Undeniably Dead Body Was Beyond Question Raised from the Dead

Now, let us proceed to the proof that the body of the Lord Jesus, which we have proven was beyond a question dead, was not only dead but was really raised from the dead. Of course we cannot give in the time at our disposal all the proof, but we can give enough of it to thoroughly convince and satisfy any honest seeker after the truth. There are three separate lines of proof of the Resurrection of the body of Jesus from the dead.

1. The first line of proof is the testimony of the Four Gospels, the Acts of the Apostles, and of the Apostle Paul.

The evidence that the First Gospel was written by Matthew, the Publican and an eye witness of the death and Resurrection of Jesus, is conclusive. We cannot of course take it up today nor do we need to. The evidence that the Second Gospel was written by Mark, and that Mark was really the amanuensis of Peter, one of the apostles and an eye witness of the death and Resurrection of Jesus Christ, is overwhelmingly conclusive. The evidence that the Third Gospel was written by Luke, "the beloved Physician" and a companion of Paul, and a scholar, and a careful and reliable historian, is also conclusive. It has recently been especially well demonstrated that Luke was a reliable historian by no less an authority than Sir Wm. Ramsey, the distinguished scholar, traveler, explorer and historian. It is one of the most conclusively demonstrated facts in Literary Criticism that the Fourth

Gospel was written by John, the beloved disciple. The rationalists have tried again and again for generations to discredit the Johannean Authorship of the Fourth Gospel, but they have been beaten to a frazzle every time and today the man, no matter how scholarly he may be, who seeks to discredit this Gospel as not being by John the Apostle, only succeeds in discrediting himself, his own honesty and candor, or his clearness of spiritual perception or his literary judgment. The Fourth Gospel beyond the possibility of honest and intelligent doubt was written by John. Now each one of these four so well accredited Gospels gives the testimony of eye witnesses to the death and Resurrection of Jesus, the Christ. There is not a single other fact of ancient history that is so overwhelmingly attested by external historical evidence as the Resurrection of the Body of Jesus Christ from the dead.

In addition to all this decisive external historical evidence of the Resurrection of Jesus Christ found in the Four Gospels, is the clear presentation of facts proving the Resurrection of the body of Jesus from the dead given by Paul in 1 Cor. 15:5–8. Now the Epistle to the Corinthians is one of Paul's Epistles that all reputable scholars, including even Ferdinand Baur and the other very able destructive critics of the extreme Tübingen school and their successors, admit to have been written by Paul. There is absolutely no possibility of honest and intelligent question that Paul wrote First Corinthians. Now Paul says in 1 Cor. 15:3–8, "For I delivered unto you first of all that which

Was the Body of Jesus Raised From the Dead?

I also received: *that Christ died* for our sins according to the scriptures; and that he was buried; and *that he hath been raised on the third day* according to the scriptures; and that *he appeared* (the exact meaning of the word translated "appeared" is "was seen," it is a word that means seeing with the physical eye) *to Cephas; then to the twelve; then he appeared (was seen)* to *above five hundred brethren at once,* of whom *the greater part remain until now,* but some are fallen asleep; *then he appeared (was seen) to James; then to all the apostles;* and *last of all, as to a child untimely born he appeared (was seen) to me also."* Now here Paul tells us that Jesus was seen after His Resurrection by Cephas (Peter). This appearance is recorded in Luke 24:34. Peter's own description of the facts connected with the Resurrection of Jesus we find in the Gospel of Mark, which is Peter's own Gospel, Mark writing for him. With that customary modesty which was so characteristic of the Gospel writers of putting themselves in the background, this appearance to Peter of Jesus after His Resurrection is not related in Mark's account. Peter's direction testimony to the Resurrection of Christ is also found in his Epistle (see I Pet. 1:3). As Paul was intimately acquainted with Peter, meeting him on various occasions, his testimony here given that the risen Lord was seen by Cephas (Peter) is unimpeachable. After His appearance to Cephas (Peter), Paul tells us the Lord Jesus "appeared (was seen)" to the entire apostolic company together. This appearance was the same night that He appeared to Peter alone, that is the day of His Resurrection (recorded in detail in Luke 24:33-36). Sometime after this appearance to the twelve, the risen Christ "appeared (was seen)" *to above five hundred brethren at once,"* that is to say he was seen physically by these five hundred at one time. That should settle the question that He actually rose from the dead and was bodily visible to men after His Resurrection. The greater number of these five hundred brethren were living when Paul spoke and could therefore be appealed to. So we see the great importance of the admission of all scholarly rationalists that Paul wrote this Epistle. Of course, Paul could not make a statement like this that nearly five hundred persons were still living who saw Jesus after His Resurrection, unless it were substantially correct. It is admitted that Paul wrote this Epistle and Paul clearly asserts that there were nearly five hundred still living in his own day who had seen Jesus after His Resurrection. Either then Jesus had risen or else Paul was a most conscienceless liar. Of course it is impossible to believe that Paul deliberately lied about this matter for Paul laid down his life for his testimony to the fact of the Resurrection of the body of Jesus Christ. And men do not give up every worldly ambition and prospect as Paul did for a lie that they know to be a lie, and endure thirty years of hardships and untiring toil and finally die, for a lie. Moreover, if this was a lie, it was one that could have been easily proven to be a lie at that time. So then it is simply impossible for it to be a lie. If anything can be proven by the thoroughly reliable and unanimous testimony of many competent

Was the Body of Jesus Raised From the Dead?

witnesses it is proven that the body of Jesus was raised from the dead. The external historical evidence of the Resurrection of Jesus Christ is overwhelming. This taken alone would prove to an absolute certainty that the body of Jesus was raised from the dead, but the internal evidence is if possible even more conclusive.

2. *If the external historical evidence of the Resurrection of the body of Jesus Christ from the dead is conclusive the internal evidence is even more conclusive.* By internal evidence we mean the evidence in the accounts themselves that the writers are exactly recording facts and not fabricating a Romance. Let me present this evidence as briefly as I can in the time at our disposal.

I shall not assume anything. I shall not assume that the Four Gospels were written by the four men whose names they have borne through all the centuries since they were written (though I have already indicated that the proof that they were is overwhelming). I shall not assume that they were written in the first century or in the second or in the third. Of course, I shall not assume that they are a record of facts that actually occurred; for to assume that would be to assume the very point at issue. I shall assume nothing whatever. I shall start out with a fact that we all know for ourselves to be a fact; and that is this, that whoever wrote the Four Gospels and whenever they were written, whether they are a record of facts that actually occurred, or whether they are a skillfully fabbricated fiction, this much is certain, we have the Four Gospels today. And we shall endeavor to discover by a

Is the Bible the Inerrant Word of God?

careful study of the Four Gospel accounts of the Resurrection and by a comparison of them with one another whether they are a record of facts that actually occurred or whether they are a fictitious narrative of things that never occurred or that did not occur as here recorded.

(1) The first thing that becomes clear by a careful study of these four accounts is that, *they are separate and independent accounts.* This appears unmistakably from the very numerous and very noticeable apparent discrepancies in the four accounts. These seeming discrepancies are marked and many. It would have been impossible for the four accounts to have been made up in collusion with one another and present so many and such marked discrepancies as we find here. It is true that there is a harmony between the four accounts, but that harmony does not lie upon the surface, it only comes out by protracted, thorough and minute study. It is just such a harmony as would exist between accounts written independently of one another by several different persons, each one looking at the events from his own point of view. It is just such a harmony as would not exist in four accounts made up in collusion with one another. If the four accounts were written in collusion with one another, the harmony would be on the surface, whatever discrepancies there might be would only come out by close and minute study. Just the opposite is the case with the four Gospel accounts of the Resurrection of Jesus Christ, the discrepancies are on the surface, the harmony only comes out by very close, prolonged and

Was the Body of Jesus Raised From the Dead?

minute study. So it is evidently true that whether these four accounts are true or false they are separate and independent accounts.

Now it is evident that these accounts must either be a record of facts that actually occurred, or else they must be a fiction. If a fiction, they must have been fabricated in one of two ways, either independently of one another, or else in collusion with one another. We have already seen that they cannot have been fabricated in collusion with one another; for the apparent discrepancies, as we have seen, are too numerous and too noticeable. But neither can they have been fabricated independently of one another because the agreements are too marked and too many. If four men should set out independently of one another to write an account of events that never occurred they would present agreements nowhere. So we are logically forced to these conclusions. First they cannot have been fabricated in collusion with one another because the apparent discrepancies are too numerous and too noticeable; and second, they cannot have been fabricated independently of one another because the agreements are too marked and too many. Therefore, *we are driven by the inexorable logic of facts to the conclusion that they were not fabricated at all, but that they must be and are a true relation of facts as they actually occurred.* We might rest the case here and call it conclusively proven, but we will not rest the case here.

(2) The next thing we notice is, that *each one of the four accounts bears striking indications of having been derived from eye-witnesses.* The account of any

event given by an eye-witness can always be distinguished from the account given by one who is merely retailing what others have told him. Each one of these four accounts bears the unmistakable evidence of having been derived from eye-witnesses.

(3) The third thing that we notice about these Gospel narratives of the Resurrection of the Body of Jesus Christ from the Dead is, *Their naturalness, straightforwardness, artlessness and simplicity.* It oftentimes is the case that when a witness is on the witness stand the story he tells is so artless, so straightforward, so natural, there is such an entire absence of all attempt at coloring and effect, that his testimony has great weight independently of any previous knowledge we may have of his character or former history. As we listen to the story of such a witness we say to ourselves: "This man is telling the truth." The weight of this kind of evidence is greatly increased and reaches practical certainty, when we have several independent witnesses all of this sort, and all bearing testimony to the same essential facts, but with varieties of detail, one omitting what another tells, or telling it in quite a different way, indeed in an apparently contradictory way, proving that each witness is telling things just as he saw them and that he has not been previously coached by some skillful attorney. Now this is precisely the case with the Four Gospel narratives of the Resurrection of Jesus Christ. Each one of the four tells his story with a simplicity, and straightforwardness and artlessness that surpasses anything that can be found anywhere else in history or in other literature,

and each tells it in his own way, and sometimes one Gospel account seems to contradict another Gospel in some detail, and oftentimes a third Gospel unconsciously reconciles apparent discrepancies between two other Gospels. The writers of the Four Gospels do not seem to have reflected at all upon the meaning or bearing of many of the facts which they relate. The great Unitarian scholar, Dr. William Furness, who certainly was not over much disposed in favor of the supernatural says in his book, "The Power of the Spirit," "Nothing can exceed in artlessness and simplicity the four accounts of the first appearance of Jesus after His crucifixion. If these qualities are not discernible here, we must despair of ever being able to discern them anywhere."

Now suppose we had four accounts of any battle in ancient history. Nothing decisive was known as to the authorship of these accounts. But when we placed them side by side and carefully compared them, we found that they were manifestly separate and independent accounts, we found also that each one of the four accounts bore striking indications of having been received from eye-witnesses, and we found further still that each one of the four was marked by that artlessness, simplicity, straightforwardness that always carries conviction of the truth of the story being related, and that while apparently disagreeing in minor details, they agreed substantially in the account of the battle, even though we had no knowledge of the authorship or date of these accounts, would we not in the absence of any other accounts, be compelled to say by every law of evidence obtaining in courts of justice in civilized countries and by every canon of reasonable historical criticism, "Here is a true account of that battle?" Now this is exactly the case with the Four Gospel narratives concerning the Resurrection of the Body of Jesus from the Dead. And if we apply to these accounts (as we certainly must if we are to lay any claim to candor and honesty) the laws of historical criticism applied everywhere else in a scientific study of history, and every law of evidence accepted in courts of justice in all civilized lands, we are logically compelled to say, "Here is a true account of the Resurrection of Jesus."

(4) The next thing we notice is, *the unintentional evidence of words, phrases, and accidental details*. It oftentimes happens that when a witness is on the witness stand the unintentional evidence that he bears by words and phrases which he uses, and by accidental details which he introduces, is more convincing than his direct testimony, because it is not the testimony of the witness but the testimony of the truth itself. The four Gospel stories of the Resurrection abound in evidence of this kind. We have time for but a few illustrations, but these are absolutely decisive and conclusive, even though there were no other instances; but in point of fact there are many others.

(1) Turn to Jno. 20:24, 25. "But Thomas, one of the twelve, called Didymus, was not with them when Jesus came. The other disciples therefore said unto him, We have seen the Lord. But he said unto them, Except I shall see in His hands the print of the nails, and put my finger into the print of the nails, and put

my hand into His side, I will not believe." We are trying to discover whether we are reading fact or fiction. Please notice how true this all is to life. It is in perfect harmony with what is told us of Thomas elsewhere. He was the chronic doubter in the apostolic company, the man who always looked upon the dark side, the man who was governed by the testimony of his senses, the habitual pessimist. He it was who when Jesus said in Jno. 11:15 that He was going again into Judea, despondently said, "let us also go that we may die with Him." It was he also who in Jno. 14:4, 5, when the Lord Jesus had said, "Whither I go, ye know the way," blurted out, "Lord, we know not whither Thou goest, and how can we know the way?" And so it is Thomas who now says, "Except I shall see in His hands the print of the nails, and put my finger into the print of the nails, and thrust my hand into His side, *I will not believe."* Is this made up, or is it life and reality? To make it up would require a literary art that immeasurably exceeded the possibilities of the author of the Fourth Gospel, whoever he may have been.

(2) Turn to verses four to six of chapter twenty. "They (*i. e.,* Peter and John) ran both together; and the other disciple did outrun Peter, and came first to the tomb. And he, stooping down and looking in, saw the linen clothes lying; yet went he not in. Simon Peter therefore also cometh, following him, and entered into the tomb; and he beholdeth the linen clothes lying." Please notice the setting of these words. Mary, returning hurriedly from the tomb, from which she had

fled upon seeing the stone rolled away from the door, jumping at the conclusion that the tomb had been rifled, burst in upon Peter and John and cries, "They have taken away the Lord out of the tomb, and we know not where they have laid Him." John and Peter instantly spring to their feet, and run at the top of their speed to the tomb. John, who was the younger of the two, indeed the youngest man in the whole apostolic company (we are not told this in the narrative but we learn it from other sources which makes it all the more meaningful) was naturally fleeter of foot than older Peter and easily outran him, and reached the tomb first. But, man of retiring and reverent disposition, that he was, he did not enter the tomb, but simply stooped down and looked in. But more impetuous though older Peter comes lumbering along behind as fast as he can, but when once he reaches the tomb he never waits a moment outside, but plunges headlong into the tomb. Is this made up? or is it life? To make it up would have required a literary skill that was not possible to anybody in that day, or to anybody even today.

(3) Now turn to Jno. 21:7: "Therefore that disciple whom Jesus loved saith unto Peter, It is the Lord. Now when Simon Peter heard that it was the Lord, he girt his coat about him, for he was naked, and did cast himself into the sea." Get the setting here. The apostles at Jesus command after His Resurrection had gone into Galilee to meet Him there. But our Lord did not at once appear. Simon Peter with the fisherman's passion still strong in him, says, "I go a-fishing!" The others say, "We also go with thee."

With characteristic fisherman's luck they fished all night and caught nothing. In the early dawn Jesus is Himself seen standing upon the shore, but the disciples do not recognize Him in the dim light. Jesus calls to them, "Children, have ye aught to eat?" They answer "No." He bade them cast the net on the right side of the boat, saying, "Ye shall find." Just as soon as the cast was made, they were not able to draw the net for the multitude of fishes. In an instant John, the man of quick spiritual perception, cries, "It is the Lord." No sooner does Peter, the man of impulsive action, hear this, than he grasps his fisher's coat and throws it about his naked form, and throws himself overboard and strikes out for shore to reach his Lord. Is this made up? or is it life? This certainly is no fiction. This bears unmistakable evidence of being carefully recorded fact.

(4) Now turn to Jno. 20:15: "Jesus saith unto her (*i. e.*, to Mary Magdalene), Woman, why weepest thou? whom seekest thou? She, supposing Him to be the gardener, saith unto Him, Sir, if thou hast borne Him hence, tell me where thou hast laid Him, and I will take Him away." Please notice the setting here. Mary had gone into the city and notified Peter and John that she had found the sepulcher empty. They at once ran to the sepulcher. As Mary had already made the journey twice, the second time running into the city at the top of her speed, she was naturally weary, and they easily outstrip her. So wearily and slowly she makes her way to the tomb. Peter and John were already gone when she reaches it. Broken-hearted, and think-

ing that the tomb of her beloved Lord had been desecrated, she stands without, weeping. Then she stoops down and looks into the tomb. There are two angels sitting in the tomb, and they say to her, "Woman, why weepest thou?" Mary is entirely occupied with thoughts of her Lord, and has no eye even for angels and wearily replies, "Because they have taken away my Lord, and I know not where they have laid Him." She arises and stands erect. Just then Jesus Himself approaches. She turns and sees Jesus standing there; but, blinded by tears and despair, submerged in her sorrow, she does not recognize even her Lord Himself. Jesus says to her, "Woman, why weepest thou? whom seekest thou?" Supposing Him to be the gardener she replies. "Sir, if thou hast borne Him hence, tell, tell me where thou hast laid Him, and I will take Him away." Now remember who it is that makes the offer, and just what she offers to do: she, a weak woman, offers to carry away a full-grown man. Of course, she could not do it, but how true it all is to a woman's devotion, that always forgets its weakness and never stops at impossibilities and thinks only of the thing that must be done, for Mary to say, "Tell me where thou hast laid Him, and I will take Him away." Is this made up? It is impossible to believe it. It is life, it is reality, it is truth. I pity the man who is so blind and dense that he cannot see that it is reality, that it is life.

(5) Now read the next verse, Jno. 20:16, "Jesus saith unto her, Mary. She turned herself, and saith unto Him in Hebrew, Rabboni: which is to say,

Was the Body of Jesus Raised From the Dead?

Teacher." Mary, as we have just seen is standing outside the tomb overcome with grief. She has not recognized her Lord up to this point, though He had spoken to her, but she had taken Him for the gardener. Then Jesus utters just one word, "Mary." As that name comes trembling on the morning air uttered in the old familiar tone, spoken as no one else but He had ever spoken it, in an instant her eyes are opened, she falls at His feet and tries to clasp them and hold Him, lest she lose Him again, and, looking up into His face, she cries, "Rabboni, my Master." Is that made up? It could not have been made up? No, this is life, this is reality, this is surely Jesus and none other, and this is the woman who loved Him. We are not reading fiction here, but indubitable fact.

(6) Turn now to Mark 16:7: "But go your way, tell His disciples *and Peter* that He goeth before you into Galilee: there shall ye see Him, as He said unto you." What I wish you to notice here is just the two words, *and Peter."* Why, *"and Peter?"* Was not Peter one of His disciples? He surely was, the very head of the apostolic company. Why then "tell His disciples *and Peter?"* No explanation is given us in the text, but reflection shows that it was the utterance of matchless love toward the despondent, despairing disciple, who had thrice denied his Lord. If the message had simply been, "Go tell His *disciples,"* Peter would have said, "Yes, I was once a disciple, but I can no longer be counted such; I thrice denied my Lord on that awful night with oaths and cursings; it does not mean me." But our tender, compassionate

Lord through His angelic messengers sends the message, "Go tell His disciples and whoever you tell, be sure you tell poor, weak, faltering, backslidden, broken-hearted, despairing Peter." Is this made up, or is this a real picture of our Lord? I repeat, I have a sincere piety for the man who is so dull and dense that he can imagine that this is fiction. It is also to be noticed that this is recorded only in the Gospel of Mark, which, as is well known, is Peter's Gospel. As Peter dictated to Mark one day what he should record, when he came to this point, with tearful eyes and broken but grateful heart he would say to him, "Mark, be sure you put that in, don't leave that out. 'Go, tell His disciples *and Peter.*'"

(7) Now turn again to John's Gospel, Jno. 20:27–29: "Then saith He to Thomas, Reach hither thy finger, and behold My hands; and reach hither thy hand, and thrust it into My side: and be not faithless, but believing. And Thomas answered and said unto Him, My Lord, and my God. Jesus saith unto him, Thomas, because thou hast seen Me, thou hast believed: blessed are they that have not seen, and yet have believed." Note here both the action of Thomas and the gentle but searching rebuke of Jesus. Each is too characteristic to be attributed to the art of some master of fiction. Thomas as we have already seen had not been with the disciples at the first appearance of our Lord. A week had passed by, another Lord's Day had come. This time Thomas makes sure of being present. He did not think his Lord had risen or would appear, but he was determined that if He should appear

he would be there and see Him. Suddenly Jesus stood in their midst. He turns to Thomas and says, "Reach hither thy finger, and behold My hands; and reach hither thy hand, and thrust it into My side: and be not faithless, but believing." At last Thomas' eyes are opened. His faith long dammed back burst every barrier, and sweeping him on carries Thomas to a higher height of faith and vision than any other disciple had reached as yet, and he exultantly and adoringly falls at Jesus' feet, looks up into His face, and cries, "My Lord, and my God." Is this made up? or is this life? This by no possibility can be the fictitious production of some masterly literary artist. It is beyond question a record of facts.

Take just one more illustration. Jno. 20:7: "And, the napkin that was about His head, not lying with the linen clothes, but rolled up (literally, *"rolled in"*) in a place by itself." How strange that such a little detail as this should be added to the story with absolutely no attempt at saying why, but how deeply significant this little unexplained detail is. For three days and three nights, from Wednesday evening at sunset till Saturday evening at sunset, the body of Jesus had lain cold and silent in the sepulcher, as truly dead as any body was ever dead. The spirit of Jesus was in Paradise, in Hades. But at last the appointed hour, the hour announced beforehand by Himself and predicted in the Old Testament Scriptures, had come, the breath of God sweeps through the silent and sleeping clay, the spirit of our Lord returned from Hades and reinhabited that body, and in that supreme moment of His own earthly life, that supreme moment of all earthly history, when Jesus arose triumphant over death and Satan, there is no excitement upon His part, no haste or flurry, but with that same majestic self-composure and Divine serenity that marked His whole career, He does not excitedly tear the napkin from His face and throw it aside, but absolutely without human haste or flurry or disorder or excitement, He takes it calmly from His head, rolls it in, and lays it away "rolled in" by itself and passes out of the sepulcher. Was that made up? Never! Never by any possibility. We do not behold here a delicate masterpiece of the romancer's art, we read here the simple narrative of a matchless detail in a unique life that was actually lived here upon earth, a narrative so exquisitely beautiful that one cannot read it with an honest and open mind without feeling the tears coming to his eyes.

There is another explanation sometimes given of the napkin being rolled up in a place by itself, and that is this, that Jesus on His Resurrection passed out of His grave-clothes and left them lying where they were, in which case, of course, the napkin which was about His head would be separated a little ways from His grave-clothes and be in a place by itself. If this were the true explanation, it would prove my point quite as well as the explanation which we have given above. But the explanation does not seem to fit the exact facts as here minutely related, as well as the explanation I have given above. The Greek word translated "rolled up" means literally "rolled in."

Was the Body of Jesus Raised From the Dead?

Now all these things that we have mentioned are little things, very little things, and it is from that fact that they gain very much of their significance. It is in just such little things that fiction discloses itself. Fiction displays its differences from fact in the minute. In the great outstanding outlines you can make fiction look like fact, but when you come to examine it minutely and microscopically you will soon detect that it is not reality but fabrication. But the more minutely and microscopically we examine the Gospel narratives the more we become impressed with their self-evident truthfulness. The artlessness and naturalness and simplicity and self-evident truthfulness of the narratives down to the minutest detail surpasses all the possibilities of art.

The decisiveness of the internal evidence of the exact and minute truthfulness of the four Gospel accounts of the Resurrection of the Body of Jesus Christ from the dead is overwhelming. Taken alone it would prove to a demonstration that the Body of Jesus that was nailed to the cross, and actually died, and that was taken down and laid in Joseph's tomb, was raised from the dead. Taken together with the External Evidence, it makes doubt that the Body of Jesus that was nailed to the cross and really died was raised from the dead, impossible for any honest and mentally and morally well-balanced thinking man and woman.

3. But we have not even yet considered all the lines of the conclusive proof that the body of Jesus Christ that was nailed to the cross and died, was raised from the dead. In addition to the External Evidence of the Resurrection of His Body, and the Internal Evi-

dence of the Resurrection of His Body, we have the Circumstantial Evidence, which of itself taken alone would be conclusive, but, which taken together with the External Evidence and the Internal Evidence, makes any measure of doubt of the Resurrection of the Body of Jesus Christ from the Dead one of the most irrational thoughts that anyone can possibly entertain.

What is meant by Circumstantial Evidence?

By circumstantial evidence we mean certain proven or admitted facts or circumstances which demand for their explanation the other fact which we are seeking to prove. To use two illustrations from the law books: A man was once found murdered; the only clew to the murderer's discovery was the point of a knife-blade which was found broken off in the victim's heart. With this clue the detectives set out in their search for the guilty party. A knife was found with a broken blade. The jagged edges of the broken blade fitted exactly into the notches in the point that had been found in the heart. Besides this there were traces of blood upon the point and also upon the blade, and the traces of blood on the point fitted exactly the traces of blood on the blade. In consequence of these facts it was held that the murder was committed with that knife. Take another illustration. A bolt of cloth was stolen from a certain manufacturer; search was made for this bolt of cloth. In the possession of a certain man a bolt of cloth was found which the manufacturer claimed was the bolt stolen from his factory, but the man in whose possession the bolt was found claimed that it came from an entirely different factory. But when the bolt of cloth was taken to the factory from which the bolt had been stolen, the holes at each end of the bolt of cloth fitted exactly upon the tenter-hooks of the factory from which it was alleged to have been stolen. But when it was taken to the factory from which the man claimed to have obtained it, it was found that the holes in the end of the bolt of cloth did not fit at all upon the tenter-hooks of that factory. On these clearly established facts it was held that the bolt of cloth had come from the factory where it fitted upon the tenter-hooks.

Now there is abundant evidence of this circumstantial character as to the certainty of the Resurrection of the Body of Jesus Christ from the Dead. There are certain proven, clearly established and admitted facts, admitted by all candid scholars, even thorough going rationalists as well as others, that demand the Resurrection of the Body of Jesus Christ to account for them.

(1) The first of these facts is the change in the day of rest and worship. The early church was largely, almost exclusively at first, Jewish. For many centuries the Jews had very carefully and sacredly kept the Seventh Day of the week as their day of rest and worship. But very soon following the Resurrection of Jesus Christ from the Dead we find the early Christians meeting on the first day of the week. Now every student of religious history knows how difficult it is to change a "Holy Day" that has been celebrated for centuries and is one of the most cherished customs of a people. How came the early Christians to change

from the Seventh Day to the First Day of the week? The apostles asserted that what happened on that day and thus led to First Day observance was the Resurrection of Jesus Christ from the Dead, and that would account for the change. No other known fact would. What is especially significant about the change is that it was made by no express decree but by general consent. Something tremendous must have happened to lead to this change. What was that tremendous thing that happened? Beyond an honest question the Resurrection of our Lord Jesus from the dead. That would account for it, nothing else would.

A very strenuous attempt has been made by the Seventh Day Adventists to show that this change was not made until the fourth century; but both the Bible and early Christian literature outside of the Bible show that this theory is absolutely contrary to the established facts in the case.

(2) The second fact that demands the Resurrection of Jesus Christ to account for it is that the one central and foundation truth preached in the earliest years of the church was the Resurrection of Jesus Christ from the Dead. The Apostles made the Resurrection of the Body of Jesus Christ from the Dead the very center of all their preaching. Every sermon recorded in the Acts of the Apostles without a single exception centers in the Resurrection of the Body of Jesus Christ from the Dead. Now whether Jesus really arose from the dead or not it admits of no question that the Apostles made the statement that He did the very center of their preaching. The apostles went up and

down the streets and in the public places of Jerusalem, the city where Jesus had been crucified, declaring that the body of Jesus that had been crucified had been raised from the dead, and that they themselves had seen him alive in His body after the crucifixion. They were arrested and imprisoned and some of them were ultimately put to death for this testimony, but they stuck to it to the end. Now men may die for an error, the error for which men die is always an error that they firmly believe to be true. In this case if their statement that the body of Jesus had been raised from the dead, for which they suffered and died, was an error, *it was error not of theory but of facts, of facts of which they claimed to be themselves eye-witnesses.* Is it credible that men would suffer all manner of persecution for years and ultimately die for statements which they themselves know to be false? It is, of course, utterly incredible and indeed impossible; so Jesus Christ must have risen from the dead just as they claimed.

(3) But the most decisive fact that demands the Resurrection of Jesus Christ to account for it is the change in the disciples themselves. Immediately after the crucifixion of our Lord we find the whole apostolic company filled with blank and utter despair, and hiding for fear; but shortly afterward we find these same disciples filled with the most dauntless and unshakable courage ever displayed in human history. We see the same Peter, who cowered in the courtyard between the houses of Annas and of Caiaphas at the accusation of a servant girl, Peter who denied his Lord three

times with oaths and cursings, we see that same Peter standing before the very council that had condemned Jesus to death and saying to them: "If we this day are examined concerning a good deed done to an impotent man, by what means this man is made whole; be it known unto you all, and to all the people of Israel, that *in the name of Jesus Christ of Nazareth, whom ye crucified, whom God raised from the dead,* even in Him doth this man stand here before you whole." (Acts 4:9, 10.) A little further on, on the same day when the council demanded of Peter and John, "that they speak henceforth to no man in this name," *i.e.,* in the name of Jesus Christ, we hear Peter and John reply, "Whether it be right in the sight of God to hearken unto you rather than unto God, judge ye: *for we cannot but speak the things which we saw and heard."* Some days later when the apostles had been arrested again and put in prison and then delivered and arrested again and brought before the council and were "straitly commanded not to teach in this name," we hear Peter and the other disciple answering, "We must obey God rather than men. The God of our fathers raised up Jesus, whom ye slew, hanging Him on a tree. Him did God exalt with His right hand to be a Prince and a Savior, for to give repentance to Israel, and remission of sins. *And we are witnesses of these things;* and so is the Holy Ghost, whom God hath given to them that obey Him" (Acts 5:29–32). Something tremendous must have happened to account for such a radical and astounding and permanent moral transformation as this. The

Was the Body of Jesus Raised From the Dead?

Fact of the Resurrection of the Body of Jesus from the Dead and their having really seen Him after His Resurrection will account for it. Nothing short of the fact of the resurrection of the body of Jesus Christ from the dead, and of their having seen the risen Lord, will explain it. That will explain it fully, nothing else will explain it at all.

Now these proven and admitted facts are so impressive and so conclusive that all intelligent and candid infidels, rationalists and Jewish scholars, while they do not admit that Jesus really rose from the dead, do admit that the Apostles believed that He did. Even so thorough going an opponent of the supernatural as Ferdinand Baur admits this. Even David Strauss says: "Only this much need be acknowledged (he evidently wishes to acknowledge no more than he is absolutely compelled to) that *the Apostles firmly believed that Jesus had risen.*" Another thoroughgoing rationalist, a great scholar, one of the most learned and able rationalists of any generation, Schenkel, says, "It is an indisputable fact that in the early morning of the first day of the week following the crucifixion, the grave of Jesus was found empty. . . . It is a second fact that the disciples and other members of the apostolic communion were convinced that Jesus was seen after the crucifixion." Now these admissions are fatal to the rationalists who make them. For the question at once arises, Whence this conviction and belief on the part of the Apostles? The deniers of the resurrection of the body of Jesus from the dead have made

Is the Bible the Inerrant Word of God?

many attempts at an explanation without admitting the actuality of the resurrection of the body of Jesus. Renan, one of the most gifted and subtle of all scholars who attempt to explain the Gospel records of the life, death, and resurrection of Jesus without admitting the supernatural, explains it in this way. He says that "the passion of a hallucinated woman (Mary Magdalene) gives to the world a resurrected God." * What Renan means is that Mary Magdalene was in love with Jesus. She went to the tomb and found it empty, and she brooded over her sorrow until she had a hallucination and imagined that she had seen Jesus alive in real fact and told her supposed seeing of the Lord Jesus to the members of the apostolic company and impressed them so that they all came to believe in the actuality of the Resurrection of Jesus. Of course this explanation is entirely untenable and shows the extremities to which the deniers of the Resurrection of the Body of Jesus are driven. The very simple and yet entirely sufficient answer to this explanation is "the passion of a hallucinated woman" is not equal to so great a task. Remember the make-up of the apostolic company. There was a Matthew and a Thomas in the apostolic company to be convinced and there was a Saul of Tarsus outside the apostolic company to be converted. Matthew was a tax-gatherer by occupation. Did anyone ever know a tax-gatherer, and especially a Jew tax-gatherer, who could be imposed upon by the passion of a hallucinated

* Renan's "Life of Jesus," p. 357.

Was the Body of Jesus Raised From the Dead?

woman? The Renan explanation can be dismissed without further consideration.

Strauss tries to account for the apostles' firm belief that Jesus had arisen from the dead by inquiring whether the appearances might not have been visionary. This explanation will not bear any careful examination. For, in the first place, there was no subjective starting point for such visions on the part of the apostles. So far from their expecting to see Christ alive after His crucifixion they would at first scarcely believe their own eyes when they actually did see Him. Furthermore, who ever heard of eleven men having the same vision at the same time, and above all, whoever heard of five hundred men having the same vision at the same time? (1 Cor. 15:6.) In other words Strauss urges us to give up one entirely credible miracle and to accept five hundred impossible miracles in its place.

The third attempt, and the only remaining attempt that is worth considering, at explaining the change in the apostles, is that Jesus was not really dead when taken down from the cross, but that he was in a state of swoon and was worked over until He was brought back to life, and that it was not really a case of the *resurrection* of His body but the *resuscitation* of His body, which was not really dead.

(1) We have already shown the impossibility of this explanation in considering the proof that the body of Jesus was really dead when taken down from the cross.

(2) In addition to what was there stated we might add, that the enemies of Jesus would take, and as a

matter of recorded history did take, all necessary precautions against that very thing (Jno. 19:34; Matt. 28:62-66).

(3) Furthermore, if Jesus had been merely resuscitated, He would have been so weak, in such a state of utter physical wreck, that His re-appearance would have been known to be not a case of resurrection but of resuscitation and it would have been measured at its real value, and, therefore, the fact we are trying to account for, the marvelous change in the Apostles, would remain unaccounted for.

(4) In the fourth place, if it were a case of resuscitation the Apostles and friends of Jesus themselves would necessarily have been the ones who worked over Him and brought Him back to life, and they would have known that it was not a case of resurrection but resuscitation, and the main fact that we are trying to account for, the change in the Apostles, would remain unaccounted for. In other words, it is an explanation that does not explain at all.

(5) But there is a greater difficulty still in the way of accepting this explanation, and that is the moral difficulty. If it was a case of mere resuscitation, then Jesus tried to palm Himself off as one risen from the dead, when He knew he was nothing of the sort. In that case He was an arch-imposter, and the whole Christian system rests upon deliberate and conscienceless fraud. It is impossible for any morally sane man to believe that such a system of religion as that of Jesus Christ, which embodies the loftiest precepts and principles of truth, holiness, and love, ever announced

to the world, "originated in a deliberately planned fraud." No one whose own heart is not cankered by fraud and trickery can believe Jesus to have been an imposter, and His religion to have been founded upon fraud.

We have eliminated all other possible suppositions. We have but one left, namely, "The body of Jesus really was raised from the dead on the third day." The desperate straits to which those who attempt to deny His Resurrection are driven are in themselves proof of the fact.

To sum up all that we have stated: The External, Historical Evidence proves to a certainty that the Body of Jesus was raised from the dead. The Internal Evidence of the Truthfulness of the Gospel Narratives proves to a certainty that the Body of Jesus was raised from the Dead. The Circumstantial Evidence proves to a certainty that the Body of Jesus was raised from the Dead. Any one of these three lines of proof taken alone would demonstrate the certainty of our Lord's Resurrection. Taken together, these three lines of argument, each decisive and conclusive in itself, prove that it is absolutely certain that the Body of Jesus that was nailed to the cross and that really died and was laid in Joseph's tomb was raised from the dead.

These "Modernists," therefore, who teach that there was a Resurrection of the spirit of Jesus but that His Body was not raised from the dead are seen to be not "scientific," as they claim to be, but silly and utterly without "the true historical spirit," of which they prate so much. But that is not the best of it nor the most important part of it. The demonstrated Resurrection of the Body of Jesus from the Dead demonstrates the certainty and historic actuality of the supernatural and the miraculous, and carries with it every essential doctrine of our glorious Christian faith. It demonstrates that our Lord Jesus was a Divine Person, that He made a perfect and sufficient atonement for sin and that God accepted the atonement that He made. It demonstrates that He is now a living Savior and can "save to the uttermost anyone who comes to God through Him." (Heb. 7:25.) It demonstrates that anyone who believes in Him instantly has every sin blotted out and is justified from all things. It demonstrates that there is to be a judgment day and that the risen Christ is to be the Judge, and that everyone who believes on Jesus Christ will receive eternal life, and that anyone, no matter who he may be or how fine his life may have been who refuses or neglects to believe on Jesus Christ and to confess Him before the world, "shall not see life, but the wrath of God abideth on him" (Jno. 3:36), and he shall perish forever.

CHAPTER VIII

WHAT ONE GAINS BY BELIEVING IN THE CHRIST WHO ROSE FROM THE DEAD

"Blessed be the God and Father of our Lord Jesus Christ, who according to his great mercy begat us again unto a living hope by the resurrection of Jesus Christ from the dead, unto an inheritance incorruptible, and undefiled, and that fadeth not away, reserved in heaven for you, who by the power of God are guarded through faith unto a salvation ready to be revealed in the last time. Wherein ye greatly rejoice, though now for a little while, if need be, ye have been put to grief in manifold trials, that the proof of your faith, being more precious than gold that perisheth though it is proved by fire, might be found unto praise and glory and honor at the revelation of Jesus Christ: whom not having seen ye love; on whom, though now ye see him not, yet believing, ye rejoice greatly with joy unspeakable and full of glory."—1 Pet. 1:3-8.

This is Easter Sunday, the gladdest day in all the year. Every day in the year is a glad day for an intelligent Christian. But the gladdest day in every year, not the gladdest perhaps in our hearts, but the gladdest in itself and in its significance, is Easter Sunday: the day in which we dwell anew upon the joy-inspiring fact and absolutely certain fact of the resurrection of our Lord Jesus Christ from the dead, the glorious certainty that underlies all the other glorious certainties of our Christian faith. So I am choosing for tonight a subject appropriate to this greatest of all great days. My subject is, *"What One Gains by Believing in the Christ Who Rose from the Dead."*

There are many Christs in our day, that is to say, there are many who are proclaimed to us as Christ. There is the Christ of Christian Science, and the Christ of Theosophy (the Christ of whom Mrs. Annie Besant descants with her usual entrancing eloquence), and the Christ of New Thought, and the Christ of Sir Oliver Lodge and Sir Arthur Conan Doyle, *i.e.*, the Christ of Spiritualism, and many other Christs; but these all are fictitious Christs. Oftentimes they bear only the faintest resemblance to the One and Only Real Christ, the Christ of the Bible, the Christ Who was born of a Virgin, who lived His wondrous life of thirty-four years in Galilee, Judea, and Samaria, Who died on the Cross of Calvary and thus made full atonement for all our sins, Who then broke the bars of death and rose from the grave and was seen alive through forty days by witnesses whom God had chosen (Acts 1:3, 10, 40, 41), on one occasion seen by more than five hundred persons at one time (1 Cor. 15:6), and then ascended into heaven from Mt. Olivet, right before the eyes of His disciples as they were looking steadfastly at Him, until the cloud received Him out of their sight (Acts 1:9, 10), and Whom Paul saw after His ascension and Whom Stephen saw "standing on the right hand of God." He is the One and Only Real, actual historic Christ, the only Christ of fact; and not merely a Christ of man's perverted and bewitched fancy. And He is not only the Only Real Christ, He

What One Gains Through Belief

is also the only satisfying Christ. Men and women may talk with glowing and bewildering eloquence of these other Christs, but after all their skillfully phrased sentences these fictitious Christs do not satisfy, these Christs of romance and fancy do not satisfy the deeper longings of the human heart, longings that clamor for satisfaction. Mere words do not satisfy no matter how beautiful and fascinating and alluring, yes, enticing, those words may be. The human heart demands reality, and Jesus Christ, the Christ Who Rose from the Dead, is reality. And He is the Only Real Christ; and so He alone satisfies. Beautiful words, finely woven into a silken or lacy fabric of matchless rhetoric, or uttered with a voice of rare melody and rich musical intonation may satisfy the eye or ear, but they do not satisfy the heart. The heart demands reality, and *the Real Christ, Christ Jesus, the Christ Who as an Undisputable Fact of History, Arose from the Dead, He satisfies and He alone satisfies.*

So my subject is, What One Gains by believing in the Christ Who Rose from the Dead.

Over and over again the people who come to this church are exhorted to believe in Jesus Christ, to put their trust in Him, the One Who rose from the dead. It would be perfectly proper for you who do not believe in Jesus Christ, you who have not put your trust in Him, to turn upon us and say, "Why should I believe in Jesus Christ? What will I gain by believing in Jesus Christ?" I propose to answer that question tonight, to tell you what you will gain by believing in Christ Jesus, the Christ Who Rose from the Dead.

Is the Bible the Inerrant Word of God?

I cannot in the limited time that we have at our disposal tell you all that you will gain by believing in the Christ Who Rose from the Dead; it would take many, many hours to do that. Indeed only eternity will disclose all that one gains by believing in the Christ Who Rose from the Dead. I will limit myself tonight to what is told us in six verses in the Bible, and even that we cannot dwell upon as we ought. The six verses are 1 Pet. 1:3-8, "Blessed be the God and Father of our Lord Jesus Christ, who according to his great mercy begat us again unto a living hope by the resurrection of Jesus Christ from the dead, unto an inheritance incorruptible, and undefiled, and that fadeth not away, reserved in heaven for you, who by the power of God are guarded through faith unto a salvation ready to be revealed in the last time. Wherein ye greatly rejoice, though now for a little while, if need be, ye have been put to grief in manifold trials, that the proof of your faith, being more precious than gold that perisheth though it is proved by fire, might be found unto praise and glory and honor at the revelation of Jesus Christ: whom not having seen ye love; on whom, though now ye see him not, yet believing, ye rejoice greatly with joy unspeakable and full of glory." In these verses we are told that anyone who believes in Jesus Christ with a true faith, that is, anyone who puts their trust in Him as their personal Savior, Who by the shedding of His blood on the Cross of Calvary made a perfect atonement for their sins, and who surrenders to Him as their Divine Lord and King the entire control of their thoughts and conduct, and who confesses Him

What One Gains Through Belief

as their Lord before the world, gains six blessings of priceless worth, blessings of such incalculable value that all the diamonds and pearls and pigeon-blood rubies and gems of every kind in the world, and all its wealth of every kind, is as nothing in comparison.

I. A New Birth

The first great blessing that everyone who believes in the Christ Who Rose from the Dead gets, is a New Birth. "Blessed," says Peter, "be the God and Father of our Lord Jesus Christ, who according to his great mercy *Begat Us Again*" (v. 3). The same precious thought is found in the twenty-third verse of the same chapter, "Having been *begotten again*, not of corruptible seed, but of incorruptible, through the Word of God, which liveth and abideth." When anyone believes in Jesus Christ he is born again, he is made "a new creation." The Holy Spirit speaking through Paul puts it this way, "Wherefore *if any man* be in Christ, he is a *new* creature (*creation*): the old things are passed away; behold, they are become new" (2 Cor. 5:17). The one who truly believes in the Christ Who Rose from the Dead gets a new nature, God's own nature, a new disposition, new tastes, new ambitions, new purposes, new desires, new thoughts, a new power of seeing the truth, a new strength to overcome sin, new affections, a new idea of life, a new will, he is made all over in the deepest depths of his innermost being. In a word, he becomes a "new man." We not only find this truth stated in the Bible, we see it demonstrated around us every day. Take George Müller for example. Before he accepted Jesus Christ he was a drunken, cheating, lying, licentious wretch. When he took Jesus Christ God made him all over and he became one of the noblest and most useful men this world ever saw, living after this for between sixty and seventy years a life of which it is an inspiration to read. He is but one illustration among millions.

I had a dear friend, one of the most honored friends I ever had, who was once a desperate forger. He had been guilty of one hundred and thirty-eight forgeries. After committing these forgeries he had sunken down until he was a penniless, drunken outcast on the streets of New York, on the verge of delirium tremens. One night feeling the delirium tremens coming upon him he went to a police station and asked them to lock him in a cell for the night. This they did, and he spent there a night of indescribable horror. The next day Jesus Christ met him and he met Jesus Christ. He put his trust in Jesus Christ, the Christ Who Rose from the Dead, and Jesus Christ completely transformed him until he became one of the most highly respected citizens of New York City. I had afterwards the pleasure of taking dinner with him in Washington at the home of the Postmaster General of the United States, where he and his wife were being entertained as honored guests. Christ Jesus, the Christ Who Rose from the Dead, did it.

The New Birth is a wonderful thing, a perpetual miracle, more marvelous than any miracle recorded in the Four Gospels. I have no difficulty whatever in believing any of the miracles of healing of the sick or of raising of the dead that our Lord Jesus Christ wrought while He was here on earth that are recorded in any one of the Four Gospels. I have seen far greater and more wonderful miracles of healing and resurrection of the dead wrought in our own day, miracles of healing of sick souls and of resurrection of dead souls. This is a miracle that we may all know in blessed experience in the life that now is, if we will only believe in Christ Jesus, the Christ who Rose from the Dead. He whom God raised from physical death can raise us up today from spiritual death, and when He comes again He will raise our bodies also and transform them into the likeness of "the body of His glory, according to the working whereby he is able even to subject all things unto himself" (Phil. 3:21).

This is a miracle that not only those who are way down in vice and immorality need to have wrought in them, but that we all need to have wrought in us. Even though you are not drunken or licentious or lying or vicious in any way, even though you consider yourself pure and upright and honorable and moral, still you are selfish, yes, sinful, and blind to the things that are eternally the most true and beautiful. "You must be born again" (Jno. 3:7), one and all of you.

It is unspeakably glorious to be born again, and there is only one way in which one can be born again, and that is through simply believing on Christ Jesus, the Christ Who Rose from the Dead. As John puts it in Jno. 1:12, "As many as received Him, to them gave he the right to become children of God, even to them that believe on his name."

II. A Living Hope

The second thing we gain by believing in the Christ Who rose from the dead is, A Living Hope. This is the way Peter puts it, "Blessed be the God and Father of our Lord Jesus Christ, who according to his great mercy begat us again *unto a living hope* by the resurrection of Jesus Christ from the dead." Hope is a blessed thing, one of the most desirable things any man can possess. Alas for the man who has no hope! The man who has no hope is ready for anything desperate and bad. It is the man who has no hope who plunges into drink and dope and dissipation of every kind. It is the man who has no hope who throws himself headlong into the ocean or blows out his own brains and those of his wife and children. But through believing in the Christ Who Rose from the Dead we get a true hope, "hope of eternal life," founded upon the Word of God. "Have you a hope of eternal life," is sometimes asked me. Yes, I have an absolutely sure hope of eternal life, not a hope founded upon the vague poetic fancies of some popular preacher, nor upon the subtle speculations of some specious but fallible philosopher, nor upon the darkened room seances of some spiritualistic medium and fraud. No, I have a hope of eternal life built upon the sure Word of God. As Paul puts it, "In hope of eternal life, which God, who cannot lie, promised before times eternal" (Titus 1:2).

What One Gains Through Belief

By believing in the Christ who Himself Rose from the Dead we get also a hope of the resurrection of our own bodies after death, a hope of resurrection not built upon some utterly unreliable spiritualistic manifestation in a darkened room, but built upon the conclusively demonstrated historic fact of Jesus Christ's own resurrection from the dead, which is one of the absolutely certain facts of history. It is a question centuries old, "If a man die shall he live again?" To that great and solemn question the Christian answers with an unhesitating "Yes."

When Colonel Robert Ingersoll, most brilliant of all modern agnostics, who went up and down the country proclaiming that "Christianity casts a shadow over the cradle and a gloom over the grave," himself came to die, his poor distracted wife and daughter could not bear to have that loved form taken away from the home to be buried or cremated; for they had no hope. Hope for them ended with death. But when Mr. Moody's granddaughter, the darling of his heart, passed away, every word spoken beside the casket was a word of hope and gladness; and when we had lowered the little form into the grave songs of triumph were sung beside it. I shall never forget the day of that funeral. Mr. Moody came to my house at Northfield and asked me if I would cancel an engagement to go to Winona, Indiana, and conduct the funeral services. I telegraphed to Dr. Chapman and was released from my engagement there and remained in Northfield to conduct the services, which Mr. Moody said his son wished me to conduct. Then Mr. Moody said, "Now, Torrey,

Is the Bible the Inerrant Word of God?

let us have no sadness here. Let us give today a testimony for the resurrection." The funeral was held out on the lawn. Mr. Moody sat on the second-story verandah of his house, just back of us. Different ones spoke, and when I had spoken what I thought was to be the last word, Mr. Moody rose on the verandah and with a calm, ringing voice, though his heart was lonely for the little one he loved, spoke words of gladness and of triumph. And when we separated there was no gloom in our hearts, just triumph in the sure "hope of eternal life" and of the resurrection.

And when Mr. Moody himself died, that is to say, when his body died and his spirit departed to be with Christ, I was again called to take charge of the funeral services. A great crowd was gathered in the church at Northfield. The casket lay open between the platform and the assembled people. Right in front of it sat Mrs. Moody and then her son Paul, and then W. R. Moody and his wife, and then Mr. Fitt with his wife (Mr. Moody's only daughter). With bowed heads and weeping eyes? No, with their veils thrown back, and peace and hope brightening every face. It was a scene of triumph and of joy. In the light of facts like these, the striking contrast between the funeral of the greatest agnostic and the funeral of the greatest Evangelist of the century, let me ask, Is it Christianity or is it Infidelity that "casts a gloom over the grave?" Faith in the Christ Who Rose from the Dead, floods even the grave with sunlight. We lay the bodies of our loved ones away for the night to sleep, but we shall meet them again in the morning, clad in new and unfading and eternal beauty.

III. *A Substantial, Glorious, and Eternal Inheritance*

The third thing that we gain by faith in Christ Jesus, the Christ Who Rose from the Dead, is a *Substantial, Glorious, and Eternal Inheritance.* Listen to Peter's words again, "Blessed be the God and Father of our Lord Jesus Christ, who according to his great mercy begat us again unto a living hope by the resurrection of Jesus Christ from the dead, *unto an inheritance,* incorruptible, and undefiled, and that fadeth not away, reserved in heaven for you." How many people there are in this world who are longing for an inheritance. Some years ago I received a letter from a stranger in the state of Washington calling my attention to the fact that a branch of the Torrey family had come into a large claim that the Government had long disputed, and expressing the hope that I belonged to that branch of the family. When I showed that letter to a relative how interested she was at once. I did not belong to that branch of the family, but I am heir to a vastly greater and grander and more enduring inheritance, and any of you may be heirs also. By simply believing in the Christ Who Rose from the Dead, the poorest man or woman here may become an heir to untold riches in a moment, in the twinkling of an eye.

Just look for a few moments at the character of this inheritance.

Is the Bible the Inerrant Word of God?

1. First of all, *It is an inheritance that is "incorruptible," imperishable.* Oh how earthly inheritances crumble! I was once talking to a lady about her sister. This sister's husband had given her for a present on their twenty-fifth wedding anniversary a set of silver plate that cost fifty thousand dollars. She never used it but once, and then a crash came and it was sold to Tiffany for three thousand dollars, to pay debts. Her husband built her a home that cost one million five hundred thousand dollars, and they never lived in it after it was finished. It went for eighty thousand dollars, and others got that. One cannot hold the most secure earthly inheritance many years. Take these magnificent homes in the Wilshire District and Hollywood and on Orange Grove Ave., Pasadena, or in Oak Knoll or at Flint Ridge; how many years will they belong to the same millionaire who built them? *"Corruptible,"* is written in large letters upon every earthly inheritance.

2. In the second place, *The inheritance we gain by believing in the Christ Who Rose from the Dead is "undefiled," that is, it is unsoiled.* Of how many earthly inheritances can it be said that they are "undefiled," unsoiled? Many of them are soiled by the way they were acquired, many others are soiled by the way they are used, and many are soiled in other ways. I knew a very nice young man who was going to fall heir some day to many, many millions. A fair inheritance was it not? No! a soiled, foul inheritance. That money was made by driving other men to the wall with unspeakable cruelty. It was made by lying,

What One Gains Through Belief

trickery, deception, conspiracy, made by methods that once nearly landed its present possessor in State's prison (and unless I am greatly mistaken ought to have landed him in State's prison). What soiled things many of these inheritances of which men boast are. But the Christian's inheritance is absolutely unsoiled, absolutely "undefiled," it has upon it no spot, defect, debasement or deformity of any kind. There is nothing on earth fair enough with which to compare it. Even the glorious sun in the heavens has spots upon it, but our inheritance is spotless, "undefiled," unsoiled.

3. In the third place, *This "inheritance fadeth not away."* I praise God for that! Everything of this earth fades. No matter how matchless its beauty today, its beauty soon disappears. You take a wondrously beautiful rose, how it delights the eye with its beauty and the sense of smell with its fragrance. But it fades! Look at it tomorrow or next day. Its leaves have fallen and are withered. There is no beauty in it. Look at a great painting. What a delight! And it can be kept for many years, but it will fade in time. Look into that lovely face. Oh, how rarely beautiful! Men rave over it. But it will fade. The fairest face on earth today will in a few years be a bunch of wrinkles, and then in a few years more it will be—Oh! I cannot bear to tell you what it will be. But thank God, there is an inheritance that "fadeth not away," an inheritance whose beauty and glory ever increase as the centuries roll on, and as the aeons roll on. Fairer, ever fairer, it grows as it approaches the

absolute perfection of the Eternal God. That inheritance is mine and it is yours and it is for anyone here tonight who will believe on the Christ Who Rose from the Dead, Christ Jesus.

And yet, there are some of you here tonight who turn your back upon that inheritance for some fading thing of earth. For a fortune of miserable dollars that will soon fade and slip from your grasp. For fame that will last at best but a few years. One night when Admiral Dewey was at the height of his fame and popularity I said, "Even Admiral Dewey will be practically forgotten ten years from now and the world will have some new idol." And so it came to pass. Some of you turn your back upon this inheritance that fades not, for the mere painted and enameled face of a "strange woman," a face that will soon be blotched with foul ulcers. Oh what fools we mortals are!

4. In the fourth place, *This inheritance is sure, it is kept in a safe place, it is "reserved in heaven."* No earthly inheritance is at all sure. I once expected my father to leave me a large inheritance. Everyone supposed he would. But the panic of '73 came, "Black Friday" came, and the hard days and years that followed. My father left only a few thousand dollars and they were swept away by mismanagement. I did not get a penny, not one penny. But I have an inheritance that all the lawyers on earth and all the devils in hell cannot cheat me out of, "an inheritance incorruptible, and undefiled, and that fadeth not away, *reserved in heaven,*" for me and for you and for

anyone who will believe on the Christ Who Rose from the Dead.

IV. Absolute Security

The fourth thing we gain by believing in the Christ Who rose from the dead is Absolute Security, not security only for our possessions but for ourselves. This is the way Peter puts it in the fifth verse, "Who are *kept by the power of God* through faith unto a salvation ready to be revealed in the last time." Now just think of that for a moment. There are many who hesitate to start in the Christian life lest they fall away again. Every man who knows himself at all well knows that he is no match for sin and the world and the flesh and the Devil. But some men have no strength at all. They are moral wrecks. But our text tells us that if we really believe in the Christ Who Rose from the Dead, God Himself, the Almighty, will keep us. No matter how weak we may be, we shall be *"kept by the power of God."* I wish I could drive home to every heart these great words, "Kept by the power of God," *"Kept by the power of God, KEPT BY THE POWER OF GOD."* Do you hear that, you poor man way back yonder in the gallery, you who have been afraid to start in the Christian life? "Kept by the power of God"? These words come to me as sweetest music in hours of discouragement and weariness and fierce temptation, *"KEPT BY THE POWER OF GOD."*

V. Praise, Glory, and Honor

The fifth thing that we gain by believing in the Christ Who Rose from the Dead is *"Praise and Glory and Honor at the revelation of Jesus Christ."* This is what Peter says, "Ye greatly rejoice, though now for a little while, if need be, ye have been put to grief in manifold trials, that the proof of your faith, being more precious than gold that perisheth though it is proved by fire, may be *found into praise and glory and honor* at the revelation of Jesus Christ." Jesus Christ is coming again. He is going to be *"revealed* from heaven with the angels of His power" (2 Thess. 1:7), that is, His glory is going to be fully unveiled when He comes again; and when He does really come again and His full glory is unveiled, everyone of us who has believed in Him will receive "praise, and glory and honor." That glorious revelation of Jesus Christ may be very near at hand, or it may be very far off, but whenever it does come we who have really believed in the Christ Who Rose from the Dead, believed not merely with an intellectual conviction but believed "in our hearts," believed with a faith that controls our lives, with a faith that has stood the test of suffering and affliction and persecution, we shall share in His glory, we shall have "praise and glory and honor at the revelation of Jesus Christ."

General Joffre has recently traveled through the land and received great "praise and glory and honor." City after city has gone wild over him. But the praise and glory and honor that he has received on these occasions

What One Gains Through Belief

is nothing at all to "the praise and glory and honor" that awaits each one of us who believes in the Christ Who Rose from the Dead, the "praise and glory and honor" that awaits the poorest and humblest and weakest of us "at the unveiling of Jesus Christ" in His glory that is soon to come. And that "praise and glory and honor" will be eternal. The praise and glory and honor that General Joffre is receiving in these days will last for a few days only. It will soon pass and some other man will take his place. As I have read of the honors and applause that have been showered upon the great General I have had two thoughts. First, one of admiration for the man whose head is not turned by these things. It is a greater victory that he is now winning in keeping humble under such extravagant honors than the great victory he won on "the field of honor" in France. My second thought is one of sadness, at the anticipation of how soon this laudation and praise and glory will pass away and General Joffre drop out of sight with all the idols of the past, only to be recalled now and then by school children and after awhile forgotten even by them. But that will not be so with the "praise and glory and honor" we receive at the revelation of Jesus Christ! That praise and glory and honor will be eternal.

VI. Joy Unspeakable and Full of Glory

There is one more thing that we gain by believing in The Christ Who Rose from the Dead, and that is "Joy Unspeakable and Full of Glory." This "joy unspeakable" of which Peter speaks does not refer to the future. Peter distinctly says that *"now . . . ye rejoice with joy unspeakable and full of glory."* Right now in this present life, every believer in the Christ Who Rose from the Dead, every one who really believes in Him and surrenders all to Him, receives *"joy unspeakable and full of glory."* I know that this is so; for I have this joy in my own heart tonight. I know what the joys of the world are. I have tasted its great joys and its wild excitements. I have had a beautiful home, I have had loving parents and have had charming brothers and sisters, wife and children. I have had money, horses, carriages, servants, education. I have been familiar with the literature of all nations and have seen the art treasures of the world. I know the dance, the card-party, the theater, the opera, the wine supper, the race-track and all the rest. I have been through it all, but there is no pleasure fine or coarse, exalted or debased, that this world knows, that is for one moment to be compared with the joy that is found by simply believing in the Christ Who Rose from the Dead, the "joy" that is "unspeakable and full of glory." Why sometimes there comes over me a joy so great I do not know whether to shout or sing or cry or all at once. It is simply *"unspeakable,"* and it is *"full of glory."* Oh you men and women who are looking for fun, for mirth, for merriment, for pleasure, for joy, for gladness, for exultation, for ecstasy, for rapture, Come to Jesus, The Christ Who Rose from the Dead. That is where you will find them, and only there. Come now.

Let me sum up the things anyone gains by believing

What One Gains Through Belief

in the Christ Who Rose from the Dead, by believing in Christ Jesus. They are: First, a New Birth; Second, "a Living Hope"; Third, "an Inheritance incorruptible and undefiled and that fadeth not away"; Fourth, a present Security from the power of the world, the flesh and the Devil; Fifth, "praise and glory and honor at the revelation of Jesus Christ"; Sixth, "Joy unspeakable and full of glory" "now," and forever. Will you come to Him now and believe in Him now? You will if you are wise. You will unless the great enemy of your soul, Satan, deceives you. Oh say you will! Look! These six wonderful things, A new birth, a living hope, an inheritance incorruptible and undefiled and that fadeth not away, security from the power of the world, the flesh and the Devil, praise and glory and honor at the revelation of Jesus Christ, joy unspeakable and full of glory, are all spread out before you. They are all within your grasp. Will you have them? Who will say, I will?

THE END

www.ingramcontent.com/pod-product-compliance
Lightning Source LLC
Chambersburg PA
CBHW050805160426
43192CB00010B/1646